MICHAEL MOORE

A BIOGRAPHY BY

EMILY SCHULTZ

ECW Press

Published by ECW Press
2120 Queen Street East, Suite 200, Toronto, Ontario, Canada M4E 1E2

LIBRARY AND ARCHIVES CANADA CATALOGUING IN PUBLICATION

Schultz, Emily
Michael Moore : a biography / Emily Schultz.

ISBN 1-55022-699-1

1. Moore, Michael, 1954 Apr. 23 — Quotations. 2. Moore, Michael,
1954 Apr. 23- 3. Motion picture producers and directors — United
States — Biography. I. Title.

PN1998.3.M65B76 3005   791.4302'33'092   C2005-904374-1

Editor: Kevin Connolly
Cover and Text Design: Tania Craan
Production: Mary Bowness
Cover Photo: Nicolas Guerin/Azimuts/Corbis
Printing: Friesens

This book is set in Minion and Meta Plus

With the publication of *Michael Moore* ECW Press acknowledges the generous financial
support of the Government of Canada through the Book Publishing Industry
Development Program (BPIDP), the Canada Council for the Arts, and the Ontario Arts
Council, for our publishing activites.

DISTRIBUTION

Canada: Jaguar Book Group, 100 Armstrong Ave., Georgetown, ON L7G 5S4
United States: Independent Publishers Group, 814 North Franklin Street,
Chicago, IL, U.S.A. 60610

PRINTED AND BOUND IN CANADA

ECW PRESS
ecwpress.com

For Uncle Bob (1940–2005)
whom I looked forward to
arguing with over this book

CONTENTS

Introduction

Bonzo Goes to Bitburg

On May 5, 1985, international media and dignitaries gathered at Kolmeshohe Cemetery, Bitburg, West Germany, to wait for U.S. President Ronald Reagan's arrival. Amidst a flurry of disbelief and rancor, Reagan had not deviated from his plan to lay a memorial wreath in a cemetery that contained the graves of Nazi ss soldiers. Lying to gain possession of press passes, and eventually past seven police check points and 17,000 members of the German Security Force, were two men from the town of Flint, Michigan. One was the son of Holocaust survivors; he spoke fluent German. The other was a Catholic seminary dropout; he spoke "fluent bullshit."

How did they manage to make it through each check point though many journalists were turned away? They used a fail-safe method as they reached the most secure check. "If all else fails, use the delivery entrance. . . . If you just pick up and carry a box, nobody fucks with you," said the seminary dropout. Offering a quick hand carrying cables and lights for the CBS crew ahead of them, the two men were let in without a hassle. The seminary dropout then approached ABC reporter Pierre Salinger to alert him to their true intentions: that they were just a couple of guys from Michigan who decided to fly to Germany to hold up a banner when the president's limo arrived. Afraid they might be lashed by truncheons, he requested that ABC keep its cameras pointed in their direction.

Salinger obliged. From the inside of a jacket, the two men unfurled a homemade bedsheet sign that read, "We came from Michigan to Remind You: They Murdered My Family." The incident made it into *Newsweek*. That seminary dropout was thirty-one years old. His name was Michael Moore.

Moore had attended a seminary for one year, when he was fourteen, but dropped out because he was forbidden to watch baseball. Moore would run for office at the age of eighteen, help open a youth crisis center when he was still little more than a youth himself, and run his own alternative newspaper for ten years — a broadsheet that would garner national attention and prestige. Moore would go on to hold a brief editorship at San Francisco's famed leftist political magazine *Mother Jones*, and to finance his first film, *Roger & Me*, by organizing weekly bingos. In later years, while touring with his book *Downsize This!* he would encourage booksellers — at the giant corporate store, Borders, where he was appearing — to unionize. He would shine the spotlight on the National

Rifle Association in *Bowling for Columbine*, and on the Bush family in *Fahrenheit 9/11* — the highest grossing non-concert documentary of all time. He would tour across the United States in a "Slacker Uprising," an attempt to incite young voters to go to the polls to keep George W. Bush from reelection. But at this moment, standing on foreign soil, hoping not to be beaten for expressing his opinion, Moore really was just a guy from Michigan. He was yet to become the persona debated over, editorialized, cheered, and satirized.

Confrontational, theatrical, low-budget, and above all, very effective, this early episode in Moore's career shows that even before his success as an activist filmmaker, he knew the power of the camera — how it can protect, and how it can demolish. As the *New Yorker* recently pointed out, Moore has been a populist from the beginning. He has also been criticized from day one — and equally by the right and left. Film critic Pauline Kael blasted *Roger & Me* — his film about the economic decline of his home-town — for omitting dates and reordering information for the purpose of narrative coherence, a device Moore has continued to use over the years.

"What was so incredibly appalling and shocking is how she printed outright lies about my movie," said Moore about Kael's review. "I had never experienced such a brazen, bald-faced barage of disinformation. . . . Her complete fabrication of the facts was so weird, so out there, so obviously made-up, that my first response was this must be a humor piece she had written."

Over the years, Moore has made a habit of exchanging letters back and forth to magazines that have disparaged him. The trend usually follows the pattern of a schoolyard fight: "You're lying," "No, *you're* lying." From 1989 onward, many have argued against the filmmaker's style, yet with each successive film Moore has more closely embraced his own definition of comedy, his own interpretation of documentary, producing visual rants not unlike the verbal rants in his books. Often his films set aside certain scenes or facts in order to construct the perfect story arc, perfect satire, or perfect political point — one meant to incite the general public to action, further reading, community involvement, or to cast a ballot. With an Emmy, an Oscar, a Palme D'Or, and a number-one ranking on bestseller book lists in the United States, Great Britain, Italy, Germany, France, Japan, Australia, Ireland, and New Zealand, Moore is not only a social leader, but the artful master of this form.

Fiction writers, as well as church and political officials, will relate to Moore's aesthetic choices, his desire for emotional arc. Without a doubt, Moore is a leader for the left, even if he pilots only via the screen and the stadium stage. Where is the actual man inside this story? Is he the same man he was when who stood on German soil, unfurling a provocative homemade banner?

It's this bravado that gains Moore his audience, and, more than likely, has resulted in this book sitting in your hands at this moment. As much as there is to question about Moore and his filmic formulas, there is much to admire. Moore poses questions that many wish they could ask. On his 1994–95 television series *TV Nation*, and later on *The Awful Truth*, Moore paid researchers to secure the home phone numbers and addresses of prominent politicians or CEOs, then made unannounced visits to them, or called them up out of the blue to ask about

EMILY SCHULTZ

policies they had put in place. He demanded answers. Often, Moore and his crews have worked their way around an issue with a façade of good will, as when Moore attempted to deliver awards to the greatest corporate polluters, or when he roadied a group of gay men and lesbians into a big pink "Sodomobile" Winnebago and drove them, discoing all the way, to Kansas to visit the home of vehemently anti-gay preacher Reverend Fred Phelps. On another occasion, Moore delivered a gay men's chorus right to the door of North Carolina's Senator Jesse Helms. Who has never wanted to phone up a politician or corporate boss at home and take him or her to task? But without access to a team of researchers, the ordinary citizen normally lacks the means to do so, or might get arrested for harassment if successful. Hence the appeal of Michael Moore.

Even Moore has suffered hardship as payment for his bravado. In 1995, his crew was bloodied as they tried to force their way into the *Detroit News* loading dock to speak to nonunion workers. In 1998, after delivering a glib "Man of the Year" award to New York's wealthy industrialist Ira Rennert, a restraining order was placed on Moore directly by then-mayor Rudolph Giuliani, barring Moore from roaming within 150 feet of Rockefeller Center, where Rennert's offices were located. Moore could no longer enter Times Square, nor could he complete his television shoots.

Searching for the person behind the liberal no-hurdle-too-high hero and the propaganda-charged villain, I sought out some of his old friends, and some of his detractors. I also decided to read everything I could find by or about Moore. What is it about this former Eagle Scout that gets citizens of numerous countries and all political persuasions worked up? Regardless of the reader's feelings about the creator of *Stupid White Men* and *Dude, Where's My Country?*, I wanted *Michael Moore: A Biography* to provide an ordered view of one of the most talked about documentarians in history.

With his baseball cap, blue jeans, Kmart-meets-farmers-market persona, I knew I would never find any answers unless I started in Flint, Michigan. Moore has traveled the world over, but he *is* Flint, Michigan. Or — as his critics might posit — Davison, the less-downtrodden suburb just outside of Flint. In fact, he is both . . . an appropriate condition for a man who has been accused of bending truth for the greater good. Since that day in the Bitburg cemetery, Moore has become not a man from Flint, but the idea of a man from Flint. In the American tradition, and the populist tradition, he holds his hometown up as an example, like Jimmy Stewart's Bedford Falls in the closeted socialist Christmas film classic, *It's A Wonderful Life*. By being that "idea" of a man from Flint, Flint's own struggles and ideals — and Michael Moore's — become those of America.

EMILY SCHULTZ

CHAPTER ONE

Just a Guy from Michigan

Inside/Outside Flint

The freeways are empty and broken. At night, their fifty-year-old arms stretch blue-veined junctions into the crackling, never-quiet flesh of downtown Detroit. Hugging the bottom of the city and quickly straightening north, Detroit's freeways were constructed for its workers, workers who drive the vehicles they have built. But from Cadillac Square — beyond which General Motors' headquarters sits in the mirrored towers known as the Renaissance Centre — to Flint, Michigan, the roads are definitely not paved with gold.

In January 1955, the Lodge Freeway opened to much fanfare. Now, even the local press concedes, "It's little more than interconnected slabs of steel and concrete. And the thing is falling apart." The day after the grand opening of the Ford-Lodge interchange, thousands of vehicles overheated in the freeway's first traffic jam — just one little example of the Motor City's lack of foresight along the way to Flint, Michigan. The Lodge is currently shut down for construction. The fastest route to Flint is the newer, though still dangerously pocked, Interstate 75. This road beelines almost directly to Flint, sixty-nine miles north — the birthplace of GM, and Michael Moore.

There are familiar landmarks. Passing through Auburn Hills, among America's most affluent counties, one glimpses the immense 1998 construction of "shopping fun," Great Lakes Crossing, complete with 7000 parking spaces. This stretch of the I-75 also offers three exits to The Palace, where if you aren't wearing Pistons paraphernalia, you had better go home. Under a milky Michigan sky, it is hard to envision celebrities traveling this same route for this same purpose: to get to downtown Flint, the original home of GM. Who has ventured along this road? GM spokespeople Anita Bryant and Pat Boone ("Mr. Chevrolet Himself" according to Michael Moore), as well as the town's own heroes, Bob Eubanks, host of television's popular 1980s' *The Newlywed Game*, and Top-40 music's billboard king, Casey Kasem. Cruising up and down the dial, there are plenty of choices — primarily new country, classic rock, alternative pop, Kasem's own preferred brand of pop, and public radio. But arriving in Flint, it is impossible to imagine the town as a destination — for anyone, let alone the busy scene-making celebs of yesteryear. True, the city has its share of Ramada and Marriott inns; the average one-night king-size stay for two is $70. But with a population of just over 120,000, a 35% decrease from the 1970 census, Flint is hardly the hub it once was.

Before the European settlers moved in, Native Americans called the local waterway, Pawanunling, *the river of flint*. In 1819, a fur trader by the name of Jacob Smith left Detroit and settled the area to the north as a trading post. In 1855, the settlement was incorporated as the City of Flint. Fur trading was followed by lumber and from lumber came the business of making carriages. After becoming the largest manufacturer of horse carriages in the world, Flint was given the name, "Vehicle City," a name still appropriate when, in 1908, William C. Durant founded the General Motors company here. Durant had spent several years buying small, failing automobile companies in an attempt to stabilize the nascent industry by monopolizing it. But by 1920, GM's main competitor, Ford Motors, still controlled more than 60% of the market. This situation changed when Alfred P. Sloane, the brilliant engineer who had made his name in ball bearings, took over GM and led it to success with a revolutionary approach. Sloane believed that, like ball bearings, consumer taste could be engineered and that, "the appearance of a motor-car is a most important factor in the selling end of the business — perhaps the most important factor — because every one knows the car will run."

With personalized brands — Chevrolet, Pontiac, Oldsmobile, Buick, and Cadillac — GM made it to the top and became the chauffeurs for the roaring '20s. By the crash of 1929, the company had seen its workforce swell to 86,000, and its stock rise to $45 a share — then fall to $3.75. Left in the lurch and dropped into Depression working conditions were the thousands of Flint line-workers who, within seven years, would make GM synonymous with the angry '30s.

Though the grievances were many and justified, 80% of Flint families were dependent on GM, and the city name was national shorthand for "company town." Newspapers, schools, homes, and government were created by and paid for by GM. This presented a D-day style challenge to the United Auto Workers union in 1936 — organizing Flint would be tantamount to converting the Pope.

But Flint *would* go from being a company town to a union town. The best organizers were sent from Cleveland and Toledo into Flint. Workers were fed up with working conditions and willing to attend secret meetings. Flint had witnessed attempted strikes back in 1930 and '34. Mimicking the sit-in strikes of Cleveland's White Motors and Toledo's AutoLite meant something else altogether. To set up camp *within* the factory was illegal — but incredibly effective. Trespassing on company property violently rankled both officials and the community at large, since it seemed to show disrespect for private property and go against the American way. The "communist" card was heavily played, but it did not stop either disillusioned workers or famed organizers Bob Travis and the Reuther brothers. Sensing the possibility of sit-down strikes, management began removing equipment from the Fisher II plant on December 29, 1936 — two days before the proposed strike. Without equipment to produce goods, workers had little hope of negotiating for their jobs in any capacity. Workers quickly organized themselves and the strike began early. Once they sat down, news traveled, and the very next day the Fisher I plant was also sitting.

Said one Flint woman of her husband's intention to strike, "He come home one night . . . and he says don't be surprised if I don't come home. . . . He says it's the only way we're going to win and he said that somebody might get killed there, but he says if I'm one of them I'm fighting for the . . . good cause."

Unlike the strikes we see today in North America with their "Hey hey, ho ho" slogans on the sidewalk, these workers were in physical danger. Treating the strike as a risk situation, they moved, literally, like an army. They quickly formed committees to attend to even the most basic of dignities, such as cleaning up and providing one another with entertainment, including song, harmonica, and cards and dice. With the precision of wwi veterans, they also formed committees for gathering food, defense, and picketing. They were so organized, many workers were able to leave to celebrate New Year's Eve and still return. During the forty-four-day sit-in, GM turned off the heat and refused to provide coal; strikers resourcefully burned bolts of burlap for warmth until management backed down. Workers were dedicated to keeping company property safe from harm throughout the strike, even though they were hearing rumors that they were at risk of being "shot out."

Like big business today, GM had the ear of both the media and the local judges. But on February 11, 1937, GM workers won the right to unionize without penalty or fear for their jobs.

By the 1950s, Flint, Michigan, was a booming, beautiful, and contradictory place. Workers had fought and gained the rights to living wages, security for their families to lead what would be known as working-middle-class lives. Elsewhere, socialists and capitalists fought over the heart of America, but in Flint, they seemed strangely at peace. Whether imagined or not, to many these were halcyon days of post-war prosperity and corporate responsibility. One Flint resident, born during the peak years of this paradise, would never forget them.

On April 23, 1954 — the year GM produced its 50 millionth car — Michael Moore was born to a Catholic Irish-American couple, in the suburb of Davison. A photo of Moore as a toddler shows him retreating from the camera, into the safety of skirts. Extended family was also close, huddling in the safety of Flint. The elder brother of Anne and Veronica (both of whom went on to become schoolteachers, though Anne later became a public defender), Michael was the only boy in the family. With his father Frank's facial features, at a young age Michael had his mother Veronica's red hair. On the edge of Flint, the world looked like a virtual cartopia: backyards led to scrub woods, and the far-flung subdivisions of humble post-war homes required transportation. The adult world moved in fleets — exiting houses at the same time each morning, and returning at the same time each afternoon. Michael's father worked the 6 a.m. to 2 p.m. shift. On weekends, the town washed its cars, fixed its cars, and talked cars. Moore, however, went to the movies, "probably three or four movies a week, five times a week sometimes." Though occasionally shy, Moore was also outgoing and took in a range of activities: fishing, the National Rifle Association gun club, and Boy Scouts.

At school he was "bored beyond belief." His mother Veronica, who had been a graduating valedictorian, had already taught Moore to read. In a true *To Kill A Mockingbird* moment, with Moore in the role of Scout Finch, he "had to sit and feign interest while the other kids, like robots, sang, 'A-B-C-D-E-F-G. . . .'" The nuns at St.

EMILY SCHULTZ

John's Elementary School attempted to skip him into second grade after one month in first, but Michael's mother protested the switch — ironically because she was afraid he would remain the smallest child in his new class — and he was bumped back again. Moore never enjoyed school, but spent his time writing plays and organizing his classmates into teams for his own covert operations: fourth-grade, sixth-grade, and eighth-grade newspaper projects, all quickly disbanded by the nuns. When the play Moore penned for his eighth-grade class was discovered to be about the rats in St. John's Parish Hall, he and his friends were barred from performing it. In protest, Moore convinced half his class to stand onstage without joining in the choir's songs. An intelligent child, and a good Catholic in spite of his occasional hijinks, Moore started to look for a career that could take him away from the factory fate. He turned to the system he'd been trying to buck.

At the age of fourteen, Moore attended a youth seminary. As a priest he would be able to communicate and speak for a community — things he had already attempted. However, within a year Moore realized the seminary forbade things he couldn't do without. For one thing, he was not allowed to watch baseball. While this may sound trivial, the Detroit Tigers had just made it into the World Series — vital viewing for a sports fan. There was also the issue of girls. Though there were no female students, the seminary band was a co-ed mix. Between baseball, these outside music sessions, and a long-cultivated dislike for authority, something shifted in Moore. He left the seminary after only one year, and enrolled in a Davison public high school for tenth grade.

By this time, the country — and Flint — was in the

grips of its greatest internal struggle since the Civil War. In 1968, General Westmoreland had requested 200,000 more troops to be sent to Vietnam, and the story of the Mai Lai village massacre had broken in the news. On the streets, a new kind of activist, typified by the antics of Abbie Hoffman, created a political theater that was equal parts vaudeville and Bolshevik. These new activists sought to pull down the pants of the establishment while launching extreme protests, such as the attempt of hundreds of hippies to "levitate" the Pentagon and cast out its evil spirits, or a bid to run a pig as a presidential candidate. Moore absorbed the culture around him. His longstanding career as a Boy Scout resulted in a presentation on the businesses of Flint — and their poor environmental practices. At the age of fifteen, Moore earned his Eagle badge — and the enmity of local businesses — with this slide show. This single act marks the beginning of his love-hate dynamic with Flint, and the beginning of a lifelong career in political provocation.

Moore felt creatively and psychologically squashed at school. "It became clear to me sometime around tenth grade that this institution was not really set up for us to learn the 3 R's, but rather the 3 C's: Consistency, Complacency, and Conformity," he remembers. Moore would grow his hair long, take up guitar, and relish the sweet escape of rock music. "I had hair halfway down my back," Moore recently recalled in an interview. "All of my friends did drugs. I was always afraid [to try them] — I mean, at that age, I felt like I was already out there, and I didn't need any enhancement."

By 1972, troop numbers in Vietnam had fallen, but the draft would stay in effect for another year. "Old enough to die, old enough to vote," was a common protest chant for youths eligible for the draft, but not yet enfranchised as voting citizens. As the voting age was amended from twenty-one to eighteen, Moore realized he was not only old enough to X a ballot, he was also old enough to appear on one. In the spring of 1972, immediately following his eighteenth birthday, he ran for public school board. At the time, he was completing his final semester at Davison High School. Before he graduated, he would become the youngest person ever elected to public office in Flint. He had one main goal: to remove the principal and assistant principal from the school he was still attending.

Not only did he get himself elected, he was vigilant about seeing things through. Both the principal and the assistant principal ultimately left Davison High. But this was only one of Moore's missions. Moore also fought for student rights and supported the teachers union. He sued the school board to secure the right to tape-record public meetings. When the school board attempted to find ways to meet without Moore present, he reported them to the Michigan Attorney General, who sent the issue to court.

As Moore watched neighborhood friends drafted to be killed in Vietnam, he gave up pledging allegiance to the flag. He wrote a play humiliating the leaders of local business. He suggested the new elementary school in the 99% white district be named after Martin Luther King, Jr. Needless to say, officials were anxious to be rid of Moore. Longtime Davison resident Don Hammond told the *Detroit Free Press* years later, "The word to describe Michael Moore is embarrassing. He embarrasses everybody." According to Hammond, Moore once sat on the board of education's meeting table, took off his socks and shoes, and began to pick his toes. Hammond recalled another time when Moore left a board meeting saying, "I don't want to sit around with you bums."

In December 1974, only two years after his election, a ballot presenting a sole question gave the public the option of voting him out. The ballot was called by petition. At first, petitions circulated, never collecting enough names. The judge extended the deadline. More names were added, but still not enough. The judge extended the deadline again. Eventually, the ballot was called — in spite of the fact that many of the signed names were fictitious or belonging to dead persons. The judge ruled that the community obviously wanted to vote on Moore's fate on the school board, and therefore, he would allow it. Moore claims the date was set during the holidays to limit the number of his supporters. But according to Moore, "It was the largest turnout in the history of the school district for any election ever held." With a 312-vote margin, Moore won the right to remain on the school board.

But Moore's political career did not necessarily begin the moment he won his first election. What gave him the time to chase big business (years before he would chase them on TV) was his decision not to enter the factory.

The entire Moore family was entrenched in the automobile industry, with parents and grandparents punching the clock for the largest company in the United States. Moore's uncle was involved in the 1936–37 sit-down strike. Moore's father Frank would work for the AC Spark Plug plant for thirty-three years. Michael would catapult his documentary career by keeping General Motors at its core, but his struggle with GM began decades before he ever

EMILY SCHULTZ

conceived of documenting the company's lack of ethics and compassion. In a factory town, from the moment a child is posed the question, "What do you want to be when you grow up?" a conundrum begins. There are the obvious public positions that children are trained to consider: nurse, doctor, teacher, firefighter, mail carrier, police officer. But what about following in one's parents' shoes?

Moore's friend, and fellow Flint writer, Ben Hamper reminisces about visiting his father's Fisher 1 plant on "family night" as a child. Unlike Moore, Hamper grew up in Flint proper. He aspired to be a poet, and avoided the factory as long as possible, but then one day, fate called. After ten years of working at GM, Hamper would suffer a breakdown and eventually check himself temporarily into a mental health facility. Having appeared in *Roger & Me,* and on the cover of Moore's first issue of *Mother Jones,* Hamper is now famously known as "Rivethead," the author of the bestselling book by the same name. There Hamper describes his disappointment at learning that working in a car factory was, in fact, not like assembling model cars from a box.

Like Moore, by the tender age of seven Hamper became determined not to follow in his father's footsteps, "We stood there for forty minutes or so, a miniature lifetime and the pattern never changed. Car, windshield. Car, windshield. Drudgery piled atop drudgery. Cigarette to cigarette. Decades rolling through the rafters, bones turning to dust. . . . I wanted to shout at my father, 'Do something else!'"

Moore's heroes were those who had "escaped the life in the factory and got out" — entertainers, rebels, and rock icons, such as "the guys in Grand Funk Railroad." In fact, Moore did secure a job at General Motors' Buick directly after high school, but "didn't even last a day."

As he recounts while discussing *Roger & Me*, "I woke up that morning. I just lay there in bed thinking, 'Man, I don't want to go and work in the factory.'" Many of his fellow graduates would enter its doors with the intention of staying the summer — and exit them thirty years later. Or, like Hamper, might have, if it hadn't been for the soul-deadening work and the shutdowns ahead. Writes Hamper, "Right from the outset, when the call went out for shoprats, my ancestors responded in almost Pavlovian compliance. The family tree practically listed right over on its side with eager men and women grasping for that great automotive dream."

Staring up at the cobbled drop-ceiling tiles in 1972, Moore glimpsed this future. He picked up the telephone that morning to say he just couldn't go in. With those two little words, "I can't," Moore put an end to a family tradition.

It was his own lay-down version of the sit-down strike: one that would change both Flint and him. Without it, Moore might never have gone on to chronicle the death of Flint — either during his ten-year career as an alternative newspaper publisher, or as a film and television director, campaigner, and author.

CHAPTER TWO

Born to Run

and the Spirit of '76

The Vietnam war is over. President Nixon and the Watergate scandal have come and gone, leaving the United States in a lassitude unlike any before. The country's bicentennial celebration is the saving grace of mid-'70s malaise. Culturally, America gears up for what may be the single most patriotic celebration to shake down the nation since the ribbon was cut on Mount Rushmore. With an eye to the past — perhaps by way of escapism — Americans break out their colors: red, white, and blue flags a-waving. In factories across the land, hot glass crystallizes, emblazoned with town names — in Keep-on-Truckin' bubble font: '76.

In a countrywide battle to "Have a Nice Day," the year 1976 trots out its big contenders. *Star Wars* — with its clearly defined good guys, bad guys, and no pesky anti-heroes — is the new George Lucas project, already in production. In Hollywood, the band members of KISS are adding their animalistic platform-tall footprints to the sidewalk outside Grauman's Chinese Theatre. The Eagles' *Greatest Hits 1971–1975* will go platinum this year, and Michael Moore's hero, Bruce Springsteen, will be seized by security for attempting to jump the wall at Graceland in an effort to glimpse his own idol. In Flint, Moore is twenty-two years old, full of spit, and ready to try just about anything available to a man old enough to have feared the draft but young enough to have missed the Summer of Love. With the capricious dedication belonging only to someone of that age, he burns through "Radio Free Flint," his Sunday morning show, a film series, and antinuke rallies.

More interesting than what Moore was doing during this time is what he has since chosen to tell the media about it (or not tell them, as the case may be). Little has been written of this period of his life, perhaps because this was a developmental stage for Michael Moore, the man who would only emerge, fully formed, as a Michigan ball-capped crusader for truth in *Roger & Me* — in other words, as a character. Even more probing articles, such as those published in the *New Yorker* and *Rolling Stone*, are limited to the one or two personal facts Moore has deemed acceptable to share during interview, in his bio notes, or via his Weblog.

What happens when celebrities — or citizens at large, for that matter — begin to self-edit? A construction is begun. Each person has his or her own idea of self, an idea of one's inner qualities, the type of role one plays.

EMILY SCHULTZ

For instance: I am writing this book, therefore I am a Writer (with a capital W). Presumably, I am alone (therefore an introvert), not always well-paid (therefore either desperate — or the opposite — moral and noble), and (one hopes) intelligent. If I were asked to describe myself, I might very well possess these basic traits. I might adopt a quiet demeanor, a shyness or coyness, show disdain for the material world, and try to impress with a knowledge of literature, art, film, politics, etc. If asked direct questions, however, I would more than likely hold little back. You could learn just about anything from me: where I was raised and what the social climate of my house was; how many siblings I have and how I feel and relate to each of them in turn; why I selected the education that I did; why I selected the lovers that I did; and what my motivations were for every career move. These are dinner party topics — precisely the problem. They are not the topics of journalism.

Journalists will report that Moore pursued an education for a brief while, attending the University of Michigan–Flint campus. He dropped out after a year, however. Here again, there's an anecdote relating to cars. Moore cruised for a parking spot one day for an hour in his 1969 Chevy Impala. Unable to find one, he shouted out the window, "That's it, I'm dropping out!" Moore drove home and told his parents he had decided to quit school. Impassioned, impulsive, and dedicated to standing by his decisions — another reading of Moore's personality might use terms like short-tempered and short-sighted. But journalists will know, or report, very little than the basic facts. The problem may be that Moore views himself as a journalist. More might be gleaned about a recent pop sensation — Britney Spears, say, or the Olson twins — than about Moore. Why? Quite simply, Moore asks the questions. When he answers them, he tends to give reportage itself — usually political. The result is a spate of blogs and magazine articles in which two reporters are present, rather than a reporter and a subject. With this in mind, we must read Moore's life story as just that: a story. Following on the heels of his brief education and catch-as-you-can activism, alternative journalism became Moore's new trade.

The house at 5005 Lapeer Road still sits on a quiet stretch of land not quite city and not quite country. With a covered porch, two floors plus a basement, white siding, and a barn-red roof, it's a house that could be the local doctor's residence in a 1940s film. It was here, where the municipalities of Flint, Davison, and Burton blur, that Moore located his next project. The Davison Hotline made this house its home, a twenty-four hour operation, accompanied by the production of *Free To Be*, the hotline's newsletter. No one answered the day I knocked on its door, but the house is now a lawyer's office that offers twenty-four hours of on-call service. Local crime in the last few years has been that consistent, a grim irony even Moore could appreciate. Billed as a "crisis intervention and personal growth organization that advocates for individual and social change," the hotline offered "a youth advocacy office, a runaway shelter, free pregnancy tests, overdose aid, personal growth groups in transactional analysis, family communications, and values clarifications, student rights assistance, substance abuse prevention, birth control information, a learning exchange program, and community outreach." While it's funny to think of Moore extolling the virtues of EST and meditation, 1976 was still a time when radical culture and politics intersected, and were both viewed as a threat to the local authorities. The *Free To Be* first issue looks typical of the age. The hand-drawn logo sits atop amateur typesetting that strives for professionalism. On the front is a picture of a man who would grace many front pages of Moore's newspapers over the next five years: folk singer Harry Chapin, who had performed a benefit that enabled Moore to start the hotline.

Over the course of its first year, *Free To Be* would grow in popularity and be transformed, by December 1977, into the *Flint Voice*, a full-fledged alternative paper. Like many alternative papers that formed in the '70s, the *Flint Voice* took the *Village Voice* (the feisty New York paper cofounded by Norman Mailer) as its model. Again, like many alternative papers, the story of Moore's paper started with a group of longhaired idealists, standing around the collective household that would serve as headquarters. Later, at the end of its run, the *Michigan Voice* (as it came to be called in 1983 when its distribution went statewide) ran a photo from their first day: an image of those longhaired idealists working to install the municipality of Burton's first sidewalk.

Authorities did not take kindly to the hotline setting up shop. Paranoid visions of underage, pregnant junkies danced in their heads. In an effort to disband the group, city officials claimed that the running of a business without a sidewalk was unsafe — making the same requirements of the hotline that they would make of any other business in the residential area. Moore had never given up a fight before, and he wasn't going to start now. Everyone pitched in, and the sidewalk was built. Thanks to the sidewalk, a moment of idealism and hope is also frozen in time.

Written in the cement is not only the rallying cry, "We shall stay free," but also Article 1 of the First Amendment: "Congress shall make no law respecting an establishment of religion, or prohibiting the free exercise thereof; or abridging the freedom of speech, or of the press; or the right of the people peaceably to assemble, and to petition the Government for a redress of grievances."

Moore would draw on the initiation and management skills he had picked up at a young age during those grade-school newspaper projects he had attempted to instigate. With the help of numerous benefit concerts, the *Flint Voice* emerged: an underground news source founded by Moore and run by a constantly morphing staff. Though Moore's friend, Ben Hamper, would become the newspaper's most famous columnist as "Rivethead," his initial impression of the *Voice* was that it appeared to be "just some hippie relic patched together by a bunch of moaners desperately tryin' to reinvent the sixties. They took themselves way too serious, and none of them had any real flair for knockin' out the printed word. 'In Times Such as These, We Need a Voice,' their cover harrumphed." According to Hamper, this motto wasn't totally unfounded. Flint was facing tough times — economically, politically, and racially. Articles running in the *Voice* explored Ku Klux Klan activity in Flint, and named Flint as the number one city in America for killings by police. By the time the paper had drawn Hamper's attention, Moore was well-known in Flint. Keeping Moore in the public consciousness were frequent television news cameos, his radio show and other radio spots, speak-outs at City Council meetings, as well as *Voice* papers decorating the liquor store lobbies and coffee shops. And continuing to find funding wasn't easy.

EMILY SCHULTZ

Moore made use of benefits to build a number of his projects over the years. Charity bingos would help pay for the *Voice* and for the 16mm used in his first film *Roger & Me*. Later, on his mid-'90s program *TV Nation*, Moore would mock the very notion of the benefit — staging a concert in downtown New York called "Corp Aid" to help pay big businesses, like Exxon, that had been hit hard by fines for their contributions to environmental disasters. But even in these early days, Moore had his eye out for his own Michigan gold mine. Flint wasn't exactly a touring destination for bands or singers, so Moore went shopping for a star next door, in the nearby city of Grand Rapids. He managed to make it backstage to popular country-folk singer Harry Chapin's dressing room, where, in spite of threat of removal by security, Moore convinced Chapin to perform on behalf of his hotline. The relationship continued through the time of the *Voice*.

At the time, Chapin had already been nominated for an Emmy, two Grammy Awards, an Academy Award, and had two gold records. He was thirty-three years old and known for doing benefits for Ralph Nader and World Hunger. So how did Moore flag down the singer of "Taxi," and convince him to help drive a small city hotline?

In an unrelated story, Hamper commented on Moore's abilities to charm and coerce: "I'd learned a long, long time ago that Michael Moore — a man who could've talked Hitler into hosting a bar mitzvah — was the absolute master of wily persuasion." Again according to the paper's own Rivethead columnist, "No less than eleven benefit concerts were held for the *Flint Voice*," netting the little-newspaper-that-could something in the "half-million-dollar range." Moore's paper had found a working-man mentor to provide it with big-dollar dreams. The country-folk singer of "Cat's in the Cradle" had found a second place to come home to. Moore was able to buy the house in Burton and establish it as the newspaper's official offices, purchasing a computer for typesetting, equipment for layout, photocopy machines, and adequate telephones. With hired ad men, secretaries, and a printer, the *Free To Be* hotline grew from a homegrown community space with a newsletter to a fully functioning newspaper office overnight.

The hotline disappeared with the '70s, but Harry Chapin continued in unyielding support of Moore and the *Voice*. The newspaper functioned for several years under Chapin's generous patronage, along with the help of many of his friends: folk trio Peter, Paul, and Mary, and also Melanie (whose Woodstock-themed hit, "Candles in the Rain," would be only dimly remembered by this time). Then, on July 15, 1981, Chapin died suddenly in a car accident. Having mailed Moore some of his writing, Hamper was on his way to his first official meeting with the alternative publisher when he heard the news of Chapin's death broadcast on the radio. Hamper pulled into a convenience store, bought a twelve-pack of beer, and turned around and went home. He knew immediately what the loss meant for Moore and the *Voice*.

Hamper soon became a fixture at the *Voice* office and a close friend of Moore's. "He took chances on people," said Hamper. "He'd call me up, tell me what to write about, tell me how long it was going to be, and tell me when he wanted it." Though the two have drifted apart occasionally, Moore has taken Hamper with him on nearly every project, including a front cover for *Mother*

Jones, a related touring circuit of television shows, an appearance in *Roger & Me*, and as television correspondent for Moore's *TV Nation* and *The Awful Truth*. In the mid-1980s Hamper's blue-collar writing won his mug a place on the cover of *Wall Street Journal*; in the 1990s, after the release of his book *Rivethead: Tales From the Assembly Line*, it pushed him onto bestseller and book-club lists. He credits Moore for his success: "I owe him my career."

By the time Hamper met Moore in 1981, "he was in no way the jaded hippie leftover I had come to envision." Hamper writes, "Moore shared my twisted sense of humor and, underneath his cocky veneer, he was just as mixed-up and insecure as I was." According to Hamper, the only major difference between them was that Moore was full of drive where Hamper preferred to knock back and relax. Put on staff as a music critic, Hamper had found something he was good at besides being an auto worker or "shoprat." It was also Moore who encouraged Hamper to write about that very thing — being a shoprat. The persona of the Rivethead was born. Meetings were held monthly in whatever living room was available, often with little accomplished, veggie dips circulating and babies in tow. Moore would ask Hamper if he was interested in writing features for his paper. According to Hamper, "I would remind him that I knew very little about the struggles of mankind and all the other atrocities that seemed to rankle these people so. Never mind that shit, he'd tell me. . . ."

In the end Moore's persistence won out, and Hamper became both author and subject of a column devoted to the auto worker's perspective. Even as he was writing his columns, he wondered who would find the life of a GM worker interesting. Moore's answer: "You'd be surprised." The Rivethead indeed became a prized writer at the *Voice*.

While the newspaper flourished with local flavor, local advertising dollars were not enough to support the print schedule. A bi-weekly paper at this time serving a community of 25,000, the *Flint Voice* veered into debt, and Moore trawled for another musical celebrity to assist his cause. In the early 1980s, that celebrity was Peter Yarrow of Peter, Paul, and Mary. According to an interview with Moore that appeared in the *Texas Observer*, Yarrow held a fundraiser for the *Flint Voice* in his New York City apartment, inviting the Big Apple's big players to help raise money for what many in Michigan might simply have called a "rag." On August 10, 1985, Peter, Paul, and Mary also hosted an after-concert party in Rochester, Michigan; an exclusive 100 tickets were priced at $850 apiece with proceeds to Moore's paper.

Of Moore's image, Hamper has previously claimed his "shop-bred genes lent a legitimacy to him being a common man." In an interview with the British newspaper *Guardian*, Moore himself said, "I believe that I am in the mainstream of Middle America." Maintaining that image has required a selectivity about how he parcels personal information.

Regarding the image of the common man, Hamper has this to say of Moore's hero, Springsteen: "The guy has made untold zillions . . . always emerging on release date as either a construction worker (*The River*), a garage mechanic ("I'm on Fire"), a minor league batting instructor ("Glory Days"), the kindred spirit of Charlie Starkweather (*Nebraska*), or some other pockmarked casualty of Crud Corners."

Finding generous icons to donate to Moore's paper was not easy, but funding was by no means the greatest obstacle the *Flint Voice* had to hurdle. In the summer of 1980, the *Voice* made national news over legal matters that went all the way to the Supreme Court when Moore stepped on Flint's then-mayor James W. Rutherford's toes. On the basis of an article about Rutherford's door-to-door campaigners — whom Moore wrote were paid by federal monies — the mayor arranged for a warrant. Flint police seized the *Voice* printing plates right off the press before the scoop could hit the stands. Moore's struggle was taken up by the Flint chapter of American Civil Liberties Union. The Flint Police Department's bold infraction of civil liberties was brought before the Supreme Court, and a law was passed in Congress prohibiting such searches.

This was not the only legal incident for the *Voice*. One of Hamper's columns, about a local watering hole called the Good Times Lounge, brought both the *Voice* and Hamper up on charges of libel. Moore was accustomed to being the center of attention — often negative, but Hamper felt more at risk. Working-man Hamper made sure he looked court-date presentable. Moore, as usual, strolled in markedly late, in clothes that looked like he had picked them up off the floor only moments before. Ultimately, the case had a humorous conclusion: the judge stepped down from the case, claiming he could not rule on someone whose grandfather had been the landlord of his office, whose parents had been good friends of his, and from whose newspaper he had purchased ad space to secure his own reelection. The delay was a stroke of luck. The Good Times Lounge closed down before the case could come up again.

It was during the early '80s that Moore met his partner Kathleen Glynn, a mother of one — Natalie Rose, who would later become Moore's daughter as well. Glynn's auto-working parents raised her in Flint along with five siblings. In addition to a revved-up love of Bruce Springsteen, and also film, she and Moore had much in common, from Catholicism to "Cadillac Ranch." The two used to sit outside Springsteen concerts when they couldn't afford the tickets, still wanting to partake of the music and the vibe.

"We didn't have much ambition," Glynn says of those days. "There wasn't talk of dreams. Maybe it was, 'Wouldn't it be cool to own a movie theater? Yeah, that's a cool idea.' Things just kind of happened." Of course, things didn't "just happen." Anyone who has worked in film or publishing can vouch that establishing — and continuing to promote — a production of the scope of the *Flint Voice* or *Roger & Me* takes natural ambition and working hours beyond compare. But that kind of admission doesn't really fit into the persona of the common man or woman.

The advertising in the *Voice* provides a snapshot of the time: vegetarian restaurants, still-popular head shops and, consistently, an ad for the University of Michigan–Flint's film club screenings. As an avid filmgoer, it can be assumed Moore spent his weekends watching art-house hits of the time: Werner Herzog's *Aguirre, Wrath of God*, a smattering of Ingmar Bergman, and documentaries like *Hearts and Minds* — a chilling collection of first-hand recollections from "grunts" who served in the Vietnam War, ironically intercut with scenes of patriotic Americans playing football. When *Hearts and Minds* was rereleased in 2004, Moore blurbed the film: "Not only the best documentary I've ever seen — it may be the best film ever."

Moore's early résumé shows that behind the denim and flannel was a workaholic provocateur. In 1976, Moore began his own newspaper and kept it running for ten years (all the while continuing his own radio show, recruiting and encouraging writers like Hamper, and sussing out celebrities to support his cause). In 1980, he lobbied against local police under the ACLU and the case resulted in new law. In 1983, he traveled to Nicaragua to learn more about that country's turmoil. In 1985, Moore flew to Germany to star in his own staging of a Reagan protest at the Bitburg Cemetery, a news bit picked up across the U.S.

In 1976, on the other side of the country, another magazine had also come to life with high ideals. *Mother Jones* was founded by Adam Hochschild. This cheeky political magazine was named after Mary Harris (Mother) Jones, a militant union organizer and socialist until she died at the age of 100 in 1930. Like many idealistic publications, some have argued once it had cut its antiestablishment teeth, *Mother Jones* had become a journal that preached to the converted, and cared as much for burgeoning New Age trends as for effective organizing and protest.

As the summer of '76 leapt forward to that of '86, Moore would become known as more than just a little guy putting out a little lefty rag. In 1986 he was offered, and accepted, the editorship of *Mother Jones*, which by that time had a circulation of approximately 160,000. Moore spent his last night in Flint hanging out with Hamper and his fellow "shoprats," Moore even going so far as to punch a few rivets himself, perhaps trying to make himself believe he could be as working class as Hamper, as working class as he must have so wanted to be.

By the time Moore was asked aboard, *Mother Jones* was trying to return to its "muckraking roots," after a brief foray into fiction and culture during the conservative Reagan years. Looking around the country for a leader, Hochschild saw potential in thirty-two-year-old Michael Moore's already formed persona as the common agitator, the man of the middle.

CHAPTER THREE

Are You Going
to San Francisco?

Michael Moore at *Mother Jones*

Michael Moore went into work and announced his plan to give a monthly column to a Flint auto worker. "The owner instead told me to run an investigative report on herbal teas. I told him I had a better idea: Let's put that auto worker on the cover. The owner wasn't amused and declared that California and I were a mismatch, just before he offered me my free U-Haul back to Michigan."

So said Moore in the narration in *Roger & Me*, the film that would follow on the heels of his dismissal from *Mother Jones*. Cofounder Adam Hochschild did indeed offer Moore a U-Haul back to Flint just a few short months after he accepted the editorship of the magazine — but looking at all that led up to the day of Moore's dismissal, and all that has happened since, it is still difficult to know what really occurred inside those San Francisco offices. Moore may have attained the position with his common-man charisma, but he and *Mother Jones* found no common ground with one another.

Though many would assume Moore was being handed the opportunity of a lifetime, he had reservations from the beginning. Taking the position of editor meant more than just a change of hats. In addition to a cross-country move, Moore was making a choice between someone else's magazine and his very own *Michigan Voice*. Moving to *Mother Jones* would mean closing down the *Voice* permanently. "I have this terrible sense of abandoning my hometown," Moore wrote in his goodbye editorial. "Well, this is it. Let's skip the clichés and the pathos and just say it was a rip and a riot to do this newspaper." Moore then launched into a list of the accomplishments of the *Voice*: "We fought the mayor and he was removed from office. We fought the Midland nuke and it was closed. We fought the Flint Police and they were indicted by the grand jury. We fought racism at Howard Johnson's/Mister Gibby's and they got nailed. We fought the AutoWorld scam and it was shut down. We fought an illegal search of our printer and got a 'shield law' passed in Congress." Moore's summation was that he and the rest of the *Voice* contributors hadn't done "half bad, considering we were usually broke, had a full-time staff of one, and could never get the hot water heater to work."

Mother Jones promised Moore a wider audience. But it wasn't all about career moves or the common good — Moore had more than just himself to think about. There was his longtime girlfriend Kathleen Glynn, and her young daughter, Natalie. For Glynn to accompany Moore, she would have to shut down her own graphic design business and engage in custody negotiations with Natalie's father. Moore would be moving a whole family, and, at the age of thirty-two, he would be leaving the only home he had ever known.

Wrote Moore's friend Hamper, "Flint for Frisco? Most locals would've somersaulted naked through a barn fire for that type of option. Not Moore. He had this goofy love affair with Flint." With California's fusion of surfer and sophisticate a sharp contrast to Michigan's homogenous quality of Ski-doo-meets-homespun, the move was sure to include some culture clash. But in that far-off clement state of palm trees, cappuccinos, café lattes, and double espressos, *Mother Jones* had primitive-enough roots: its original offices were located above a McDonald's. It was an April day in 1976 when Hochschild, alongside cofounders Paul Jacobs and Richard Parker, opened the box of the first very first print run of *Mother Jones*. The smell from the deep fryer below wafted up to mingle with their excitement as they passed copies around and marveled at their newly realized forum for confronting major business, environmental misconduct, and the country's dirtiest politics.

Hired in April ten years later, Moore was given a warm and glowing welcome in the June issue of *Mother Jones* by Hochschild himself. According to Hochschild, he and publisher Don Hazen, departing editor Deirdre English, and art director Louise Kollenbaum "interviewed several dozen journalists from one side of the country to the other. We considered candidates from other national magazines, from major publishing houses, and from several of the country's best-known newspapers. But the choice we finally made was a bold and daring one, somebody who came from none of those worlds."

What followed was the biography of Moore that you already know by rote: a life in Flint, the son of an auto worker, the nephew of a 1937 sit-down striker, an elected official at the age of eighteen, founder of the *Michigan Voice*. Hochschild called the *Voice* remarkable, pointing out that it was "the only such paper in the United States with its roots in a working-class community." He went on to joyously declare, "From six feet under her gravestone in Mount Olive, Illinois, came the muffled voice of Mary Harris Jones (1830–1930), from whom we take our name: 'Hire that young feller!'"

It's no wonder that staff at *Mother Jones* were excited about Moore. He stood for everything the magazine was meant to embody. In the magazine's own words, Mary Harris "Mother" Jones "crafted a persona that made her a legend among working people." Mary Harris was Irish-born, and ten years old when her family, survivors of the potato famine, immigrated to Canada. In Toronto, she studied dressmaking, then went on to become a teacher, a career that took her to Monroe, Michigan, and eventually Chicago and Memphis. She met her husband George Jones, an iron worker, on the eve of the Civil War; they married that same night. The two of them survived the war to have four children — all of whom died of yellow fever, as did George. Harris Jones was suddenly alone, only thirty years old. She returned to Chicago to resume a career in dressmaking, but her shop burned in the fire of 1871. Twenty-five years later she was still poor, struggling to survive. She found strength inventing herself, initially, as a local character. By 1900, people had ceased to

EMILY SCHULTZ

call her Mary, referring to her instead as "Mother." In addition to dressing in antique black frocks, she embellished her age. According to a *Mother Jones* profile of Mother Jones the woman, "by casting herself as the mother of downtrodden people everywhere, Mary Jones went where she pleased, spoke out on the great issues of her day, and did so with sharp irreverence. . . . Paradoxically, by embracing the very role of family matriarch that restricted most women, Mother Jones shattered the limits that confined her."

As Harris Jones used the constraints of the ultimate female figure to raise herself (and her "children") up, so Moore uses to his advantage (and to his neighbors' advantage) the trait with the greatest potential to keep him down: his down-at-heel birthright, the face of the working class. The difference between Moore and Harris Jones was that she grew into her persona late in life; his appears to have been manifest nearly at birth. Unfortunately for Moore, *Mother Jones* the magazine did not long continue to believe in the similarities between the two.

When Moore boarded the masthead of *Mother Jones*, some of the nation's — and the world's — most recognized lefty writers were already among its ranks: Barbara Ehrenreich was a regular columnist; Christopher Hitchens, a contributor; and David Talbot, a senior editor who would leave upon Moore's appointment and go on to found and edit online magazine *Salon. Mother Jones* itself had been founded on the heels of the Nixon scandal, and had no qualms about exposing other scandals. In 1977, the first exposé of the Ford Pinto's bad habit of combusting when rear-ended in basic fender-benders was scouted and penned by *Mother Jones'* business manager on a tip from an insurance investigator. That story brought *Mother Jones* into the mainstream limelight. By 1986, *Mother Jones* was holding on to that mainstream audience as much as it could; the July/August issue shows a fed-up letter from a reader insulted by the magazine's "crass commercialism" — a sweepstakes campaign and free doormat as a means for raising subscription numbers.

Fighting for control of the advertising pages were a variety of activist groups, such the National Abortion Rights Action League, Peace Development Fund, Fund for Renewable Energy and the Environment (in regard to Chernobyl), and Nicaragua Medical Aid, as well as charities that yanked hard at the heartstrings with seas of sad faces: Save the Children, and Holy Land Christian Mission International. Caught between these do-good factions of advertisers were the middle-class trends of the time: the "backless" back chair, wrinkly toy animals known as Shar-Pei Plush Puppies, Soloflex workout, Chi pants, Sato Sweetheart Watches, Birkenstock sandals, catalogues from Good Vibrations and the Nature Company, not to mention Gary Larsen *Far Side* T-shirts, handcrafted unicorn figurines, and other landfill. If the advertisers were any indication, *Mother Jones*, like the political left in North America in general, was going through a time of change and did not know quite what it wanted to be.

On August 1, the advertising at *Mother Jones* ignited the first major row among new editor Moore, publisher Hazen, and founder Hochschild. A new addition to the advertising staff found himself terminated after his second day. Moore opposed the firing. A month later, Moore found himself terminated. *Mother Jones* claimed it had nothing to do with the firing of the ad person, whose name was Richard Schauffler. Moore claimed it did, among other things. From this point on, there were as many versions of the truth as there were people strolling the magazine's offices.

According to the *New York Times*, September 5 was the date Moore was informed he would have to give up his position. According to *The Nation*, Moore was informed of his dismissal on September 2, his now-adopted daughter Natalie's first day of school. *The Nation* editorial was by none other than Alexander Cockburn, one of the rising stars of New Journalism in the 1980s. After a dismissal from the *Village Voice*, Cockburn wrote regularly for *The Nation* and for the *Wall Street Journal*. He had written for *Mother Jones*, both under Moore's editorship and earlier. In his September 13 *The Nation* column, titled "Beat the Devil," Cockburn set up Moore as the common man, contrasting him to millionaire owner Hochschild in a vicious poor vs. rich struggle. Of Hochschild, he wrote, "Hochschild is heir to the AMAX mining fortune, and although he has devoted substantial amounts of the family income, originally generated by African wage-slaves, to finance the quasi-liberal periodical *Mother Jones*, he can still behave like a nineteenth-century mill owner." Of Moore he wrote, "Michael Moore is not rich, and before he came to San Francisco last spring he ran a fine weekly paper, the *Michigan Voice*, out of Flint, which is where he grew up, the son of an auto worker. . . ." Cockburn went on to point out that a "tough working-class editor," had been sought for the position, one who "foolishly, as it turned out, believed the P.R. which was in fact a short-term romantic fantasy of the well-heeled recruiters of *Mother Jones*."

Moore did not run a weekly paper as Cockburn stated (the *Flint Voice* had been bi-weekly, and the *Michigan Voice* was, in fact, a monthly), and ad rep Schaufler, who was referenced further on in this column, would become, by October 4 and from Cockburn's own pen, Schauffler with two *fs*. According to the original Cockburn column, the contested Schauffler was fired because of his previous political connection to the Democratic Workers Party, for whose publishing arm he had also sold advertising, something he said he had made clear in his interview with *Mother Jones* prior to his hiring. Cockburn wrote, "Moore said he could not support the action, in which Schaufler was victimized for his political past." Schauffler himself filed grievances with the District-65 United Auto Workers, the union that represented *Mother Jones* employees. According to the *New York Times* on September 27, "Don Hazen, publisher of *Mother Jones*, said Mr. Schauffler's dismissal was a 'business decision' because Mr. Schauffler's past affiliation would have made him ineffective as an advertising salesman."

Hochschild wrote a letter to *The Nation*, which ran on October 4. It refuted the arguments put forth in Cockburn's column, but did not address the issue of the firing of Schauffler. Nor did an October 4 letter signed by a long list of *Mother Jones'* senior staff, including publisher Don Hazen, address the issue of Schauffler's dismissal. Hochschild, Hazen, and company were more concerned with addressing statements made by Cockburn relating to the magazine's circulation numbers, management, vision, and one particular feature by a writer named Paul Berman.

All sides agree that Berman, who had written a feature

on Nicaragua that had been published earlier that year, and was meant to publish a follow-up or second part to the feature under Moore's editorship, was a point of contention between Moore and Hochschild. Everyone also agrees Moore refused to run the follow-up feature, for which the magazine had already heavily paid in travel expenses. But no one agrees whether Moore's initial refusal to run the piece figured into his firing. I was able to contact a member of the *Mother Jones* staff from that time, who agreed to be interviewed providing anonymity was assured. This source confirmed, "Michael did not feel an article critical of the Sandinistas had any place in the magazine, and was not going to run it. And there was certainly a disagreement about that, because others felt that the fact that it was not totally supportive of Ortega was not a reason that it should not appear in the magazine." The editor later agreed to publish it, accompanied by a counterpoint editorial that Hochschild suggested either Moore or Cockburn provide.

Of the Berman article, Cockburn quoted Moore as saying, "Reagan could easily hold it up, saying, 'See, even *Mother Jones* agrees with me.' The article was flatly wrong and the worst kind of patronizing bullshit. You would scarcely know from it that the United States had been at war with Nicaragua for the last five years." Cockburn attributed to Hochschild the sentiment that it was best "to stay out of bed with revolutionary movements."

Bear in mind that public in-fighting among lefty critics has a long tradition. Also, the situation with Nicaragua and the U.S. at this time was at its most inflamed and polarizing. Demonizing the small country as the next Cuba, in July of 1986, President Reagan, the Senate, and the House had voted $100 million in military assistance to the Contras, a guerilla force trying to overthrow the communist Sandinista government headed by Daniel Ortega. The Sandinistas themselves had overthrown the conservative government headed by Anastasio Somoza. The Contras, it was widely reported, were trained by the CIA in methods of torture — skills that many, including Amnesty International, believed were put into practice. After aid to the Contras was outlawed later in the '80s, the Reagan administration was almost brought down after it was revealed that funding was still occurring through Byzantine networks involving arms sales to Iran.

Hochschild felt there were more battles occurring than just those south of the U.S. In his refutation of Cockburn's column, he claimed Cockburn made "a number of flights from reality, the chief of which is that he twists everything into his own longstanding politico-literary feud with writer Paul Berman." Regarding the actual article in question, Hochschild wrote, "Part one was published in the magazine earlier this year: a reporting piece that said the Contra war against the Sandinistas was basically a war of the rich against the poor — a conclusion that should satisfy even Cockburn." Part two, Hochschild clarified, "continues a basically sympathetic look at Sandinismo, but says its Marxism-Leninism has proved an instrument better for overthrowing Somoza than for managing an economy." Admitting to a disagreement with Moore over the article's length, Hochschild wrote that he insisted that Moore run the article for the following reasons: a commitment had been made; Hochschild believed the article to be interesting; and a writer should have the freedom to raise "a partly critical perspective on something the magazine and he generally support, like the Nicaraguan revolution." Bitingly, he added, that unlike Cockburn, he did not believe in sacred cows.

Hochschild also stated that he had never raised the issue of the Berman article as a reason for Moore's being let go. "Cockburn also implies there was something duplicitous about my not describing these reasons to Cockburn. I felt it was no service to Moore to describe why most people at *Mother Jones* felt he had not succeeded as editor."

Publisher Hazen, art director Louise Kollenbaum (who had been with the magazine since its inception), managing editor Bruce Dancis, associate publisher Dirk Bunce, senior editor Bernard Ohanian, advertising director Roberta Orlando, and business director David Assmann all signed their names to a letter to *The Nation* that *did* provide reasons: "Michael Moore's lack of success at *Mother Jones* had nothing to do with his politics; in fact it was the intensity of his political passion that led us all to have high hopes for him in the first place." They continued, "Like many people who have not met the expectations of their coworkers, Moore apparently tries to find someone else to blame, and an evil motive behind his fall from grace — even when there is none." Their letter accused Moore of choosing to "obscure his problems as editor by raising noble causes like the Sandinistas and the rights of labor." They qualified that Moore's lack of success as editor had more to do with "his performance on the job, his relations with his coworkers and his inability to bring to the magazine the caliber of stories he so eloquently promised."

This team also pointed out that Moore had canceled two out of three of the magazine's meetings to attempt a settlement following his termination. By this point, however,

Moore had long ago filed a $2 million suit against *Mother Jones*, charging the magazine with fraud and breach of contract. Hochschild had offered him two months' salary and a moving truck back to Flint, along with an end-of-the-week time frame to pack up his office. Just as Moore had taken his story to Cockburn the very next day, he had also filed his suit promptly (five days after his dismissal, according to the *New York Times*). "The magazine is damaging itself — I'm not damaging the magazine," Moore said.

My anonymous *Mother Jones* source said, "I think it got portrayed as a struggle between Michael and Adam Hochschild. If you were a receptionist or an intern or a researcher or somebody on the lower end of the totem pole, [Michael] treated you very nicely. He was magnanimous. He was a really good guy. But a lot of the problems happened because he couldn't . . . If there were a staff meeting, and one of the other editors or publisher, or one of the other management people would say something, he'd just say, 'Well, that's the dumbest thing I've ever heard in my life. Why would you say that?' I mean, right in front of them. He did that repeatedly." Though this staff member never had any problems with Moore, the source said, "it was as if he had a hard time with other people who were to be treated as his equals. He seemed to feel it was necessary to mock them to their face in front of the whole staff." According to this source, "after three months, the managers and other editors were *begging* Adam Hochschild to do something. When he finally did, it was portrayed as this battle between Adam, who couldn't stand to have an actual working class guy running his magazine, and Michael Moore. And that really wasn't the way it went down."

"I think, whatever you say about Michael," my anonymous source confided, "people who have worked with him generally didn't find him easy to work with." This former coworker was quick, however, to defend Moore on what he went on to accomplish, saying, "I liked him a lot until after all of this happened. And I still can't help but be intrigued by him, and be really very glad he's doing what he's doing. I think he's kind of put the *Mother Jones* thing behind him pretty thoroughly at this point, and really gone on and done his thing very effectively."

Cockburn continued to disagree with *Mother Jones'* staff in a printed war of words. He claimed that when Hochschild informed the magazine's staff of Moore's departure, he cited the Berman dispute — and that this had been confirmed to Cockburn by a member of the staff who was present. "Michael's account of the conversation he had with Adam was quite different from Adam's account of it," said my anonymous source impartially. Cockburn again brought up Schauffler, including accusations of "smears" by *Mother Jones* using Teamster friends on the UAW union that was handling Schauffler's grievance. Cockburn denied having participated in anything as grand as a "feud" with Berman. Moreover, Cockburn's opinion on the entire Moore debacle was as follows: "The line now put forth by Hochschild and sidekicks is that there was nothing 'political' in Moore's firing. It's hard to know what the word 'political' means to these people . . . Hochschild hired Moore to change things; Moore believed him and came west and put his foot in it right away. . . ."

Cockburn referenced an article by Katy Butler for the *San Francisco Chronicle*. She had written, "First, senior staff members say [Moore] started his new job by launching a tactless attack on recent issues and was surprised when present and former staffers ganged up on him." Cockburn sarcastically responded, "Well, you can tell right there that the man was impossible." According to Cockburn, Moore's "tactless attack" included his dislike of a fawning cover story on Joe Kennedy Jr. "This was heard with deep displeasure by the sponsors of the Kennedy story," wrote Cockburn, "including departing editor (and extant influence) Deirdre English, managing editor Bruce Dancis and others, who began to develop the very definite idea that this Moore wasn't the ticket after all. Nothing political, of course."

Moore had a few supporters after all. The saga continued in the October 11 issue of *The Nation* with a letter from less-than-senior staff of *Mother Jones*, who did not want the public to think that the entire magazine was represented by the undersigned in the previous issue of *The Nation*. Signed by eleven employees representing several departments, these employees wrote, "in fact, a careful survey of the *Mother Jones* staff would reveal a wide range of opinion." Acknowledging that they were divided by the issue, they still chose to close their letter on a positive note: "Finally, many of us feel that hiring Moore was a bold move for the magazine, we hope that the next hiring will be as bold."

Berman himself had a few choice words to contribute, and ran a rebuttal in the *Village Voice*, including the suggestion that Moore himself was "doing Reagan's work" by suing *Mother Jones*. The Reagan insult was batted back and forth with the intensity and frequency of a tennis ball — from publication to publication and player to player.

EMILY SCHULTZ

But Moore had no intention of going quietly. If *Mother Jones* had hoped he would slink back to Flint without a peep, they obviously *had* hired the wrong editor. Though he eventually did head back to Michigan, Moore first staged a press conference outside San Francisco City Hall, where he read aloud from Berman's unpublished article. According to my anonymous source, the press conference was "to announce his lawsuit against *Mother Jones*, which was . . . two million dollars or something. I'm not sure what it was, but in the end, he settled with our insurance company for roughly $52,000." With such a national brouhaha, *Mother Jones* decided to confront the scandal within their own pages. In December, Hochschild took the reigns temporarily as editor, ran an editorial on the magazine's "family" troubles, and also ran the offending Berman article as planned, without a counterpoint article by Cockburn, Moore, or anyone else.

There were opinions on the Moore/*Mother* breakup even back in Michigan. As Hamper wrote in *Rivethead*, "the publisher also accused Moore of never being around the office or, for that matter, the state of California. Mike was rather adept at concocting any excuse to fly back to Flint. But doing battle with that procession of poseurs, who could blame him?" Hamper survived Moore at *Mother Jones* by one issue.

Because the magazine worked a month ahead of schedule, by the time the October issue was due on stands, Moore was already embroiled in the fallout. The *Mother Jones* issue had already gone to press when the hubbub emerged in *The Nation*. Side by side on newsstands, Moore's *Mother Jones* editorial was still pontificating on his vision for the magazine: how he considered it the press's responsibility to "comfort the afflicted and afflict the comfortable;" how when he looked out his *Mother Jones* office window he gazed across the street at a welfare lineup on Mission Street, a scene not unlike what Moore had left behind in Flint; how he intended to bring on board another Michigan writer besides Hamper; and how he hoped *Mother Jones* would pick up popularity in the Flints and Clevelands of the country. In the November issue, Hamper's column criticizing Bruce Springsteen and John Cougar Mellencamp for co-opting the image of the working class saw print, though Moore's absence was obvious.

It should be noted that Moore and Hamper had done a good deal of promotion for Moore's first issue; the Rivethead had flown to San Francisco on the magazine's dime, and the two had completed a full interview circuit together. Then Hamper flew to Chicago without Moore — opting instead to take coworker Dave — to appear on a television segment. The letters, or "Back Talk," in the magazine were full of mixed reviews for both the Rivethead and Moore — but that was nothing new for *Mother Jones*. Its readers were usually quick to point out errors in reporting, or to weigh in with opposing opinions. Of Hamper's presence in the magazine, my anonymous source stated, "I think people liked it. I certainly don't remember any grumbling about that. It was a really unusual perspective of factory life from the point of view of a pretty articulate worker."

Moore told Hamper that bringing him aboard as a regular columnist hadn't earned him any points with the publisher, and that Hazen had been particularly offended by Hamper's review of the *Faces of Death* documentary trilogy. However, the very same week, the managing editor extended his praise to Hamper in a letter that requested the Rivethead stay on as a *Mother Jones* columnist in spite of Moore's firing. Hamper chose to remain neutral on all fronts: he kept his head low and close to home, going back to editor Kathy Warbelow, who had previously offered him a column at the *Detroit Free Press*' Sunday magazine. Her offer still stood and the Rivethead continued his chronicles.

Looking at the issues bearing Moore's name on the masthead, one can assume that much of the content was inherited from its former editor; the first issue bears the standard *Mother Jones*' tone and direction (i.e. "Saturday Morning Fever: The Commercialization of Cartoons"). Standing out proudly from the first issue, though, is the grinning mug of Hamper on the cover, and Hamper's stream-of-consciousness assembly-line writing. Unlike the rest of the writing in the issue, the Rivethead piece moves slowly — at the pace of cars inching down the line — and has a colloquial tone as funny as it is raw. It's easy to see why Moore fought hard for the column's inclusion. The smart, disaffected man from middle America was an image Moore knew he could harness for himself and the magazine.

Using the eventual settlement as seed money, Moore would segue from the *Mother Jones* disaster into a great success with his film, *Roger & Me*. But Cleveland Park, Washington D.C., was the next stop on his list, where he would write for Ralph Nader's media newsletter. Coming to Nader's attention in the fallout from *Mother Jones*, in just two short months, Moore burned through two cities and two jobs. Another fallout — this time with Nader —

sent Moore home to Flint, with Glynn and Natalie in tow. According to Moore, he had been given a substantial advance to write a book on General Motors, and, in an interview with the *New Yorker*, Moore said that Nader jealously dismissed him. According to the Nader organization, Moore failed to report to work. At first, Moore was depressed about both dismissals. He did little but sleep and venture out to see cheap movies. Between these discount matinées and Roger Smith's announcements of lay-offs, Moore found film as a form — and it became his purpose. "I can't heap enough praise on the publisher of *Mother Jones* for firing me," Moore said years later. "Otherwise, I never would have made *Roger & Me*." In the smash hit documentary, the *Mother Jones* incident would only come up as a casual aside. But in 1997, old wounds would reopen in the new medium of the Internet.

An article on *Salon* by Daniel Radosh entitled "Moore Is Less," was one of the first pieces of absolutely malicious journalism aimed at Moore in the wake of his success with *Roger & Me*, *TV Nation*, his one fictional film credit, *Canadian Bacon*, his documentary of his book tour and an attack on Nike known as *The Big One*, and, in particular, his bestselling book, *Downsize This!* Putting Moore on par with Rush Limbaugh and Howard Stern, Radosh pointed out, "for most people on the left, Moore is welcome news. Some of us, however, have had enough." Claiming the left had often supported Moore because he was "in service of a larger truth," Radosh poked fun at every accomplishment in Moore's career, including personal taunts at his sense of humor: "Hey Mike, for your next book: airline peanuts, and how hard they are to open. It'll *kill*." Radosh criticized Moore's working relationship with his staff, particularly writers on *TV Nation*. "On another Moore project, one senior staffer regularly responded to Moore's abuse by presenting the boss with a big box of doughnuts. He assured coworkers he was not trying to placate Moore. Rather, he figured Mike's intemperate scarfing would hasten the fat man's death." Radosh didn't stop there. Most important, perhaps, was his charge that Moore's writers were dissuaded from joining the Writers Guild, and that those who did often had to rely on the Guild to secure their payments.

Moore fired back. Calling the article "libelous," particularly on the accusation regarding the Writers Guild, Moore took a few cheap shots of his own, namely at the sexuality of *Salon*'s editor and founder David Talbot. Talbot, who penned a book in the '80s called *Burning Desires: Sex in America*, was at one time part of the free love movement of San Francisco. In fact, Talbot was so liberal about everything in his life, that were it not for his California upbringing and sexual experimentation, he might very well resemble the young always-stirring-things-up politico that we associate with Moore.

Talbot was raised in Hollywood. His father, Lyle, was a famous character actor with roles on *Ozzie and Harriet* (Joe Randolph), and in cult films like Ed Wood's *Glen or Glenda*. Talbot's brother played Gilbert, a friend to the Beave on *Leave It to Beaver*. Talbot himself never acted, opting instead for activism. He was kicked out of Harvard Preparatory School in the '60s for turning the school literary magazine into an anti-Vietnam War pamphlet. A "disciplinary risk" in spite of his good grades, Talbot could only get into one college: hippie hangout University of California–Santa Cruz. In addition to his work at

Mother Jones, where he was a lefty who always ran slightly at odds with the left, Talbot worked for the *San Francisco Examiner* alongside other "rogue" figures like Hunter S. Thompson. There, working for a mainstream newspaper, Talbot was among the first to extol the virtues of feminist theorist Camille Paglia, running an infamous photograph of her dressed in bondage gear inside a porn shop. As much as Moore has been dubbed a populist, Talbot has been known as a sensationalist.

More significant than a one-line swipe at Talbot's sexual scholarship, which Moore called "embarrassing," was Moore's dredging up of the *Mother Jones* days. Moore told *Salon*'s readers, "you should know that *Salon*'s editor, David Talbot, resigned in protest in 1986 when I was chosen over him to become the new editor of *Mother Jones* magazine, where he was senior editor at the time. . . . David, it's been eleven years — get over it." Talbot had been on staff at *Mother Jones* in 1986, and had indeed applied for the job of editor, which went to Moore.

Moore then addressed each of Radosh's points by citing his own awards and credentials, concluding with these thoughts on wealth: "Daniel Radosh grew up living the charmed life in the literary circles of Manhattan. He goes on and on about how I now live there, as if this is some indication that I am no longer working class." Expecting an instant win, Moore pulled out the class card, "What's really bothering him, I think, is that one of 'them' (i.e., me) has moved into the neighborhood. Oooh, scary! A guy who's supposed to be building Buicks in Flint is now prowling the streets that were paved for the Daniel Radoshes of the world. . . . Protect the Starbucks!"

Radosh wrote back refuting his supposed charmed

Manhattan upbringing, voicing his disappointment that his "proud Brooklyn childhood of stoopball and *Welcome Back Kotter*" had been transformed into "tedious evenings at Elaine's with Norman Mailer."

Talbot refuted Moore's charge of a longstanding jealousy thusly: "Despite Moore's charges of sinister conspiracy, *Salon* never plotted to attack him out of personal or corporate malice." Talbot admitted he had personally enjoyed *Roger & Me*, and pointed out that after Moore's book, *Downsize This!*, was published, Moore had been asked to appear on the *Salon* cover — but canceled the interview. Talbot wrote that as a very public voice of lefty politics and labor causes, Moore had "opened himself up to press criticism by developing a reputation as a bullying boss. (The fact that he has built a cushy life for himself in Upper Manhattan by hectoring America's plutocrats also makes him a worthy target, as the social satirist in Moore would be the first to appreciate.)"

Talbot denied he had ever held a grudge against Moore, and reiterated that he had been ready to join Moore in solidarity after the *Mother Jones* firing — until he realized the issue went beyond management. Talbot said he decided not to attend Moore's City Hall press conference after he "heard directly from many of *Mother Jones'* aggrieved employees that it was not just the owner who was fed up with Moore, but much of the magazine's staff as well, who found him to be an autocratic and incompetent manager."

While this He Said/He Said does little to illuminate what really happened between the spring and fall of 1986 at *Mother Jones*, it does show how Moore dealt with difficulties in his life. In five short months, Moore had come to prominence among the American left and learned that the rules governing media were far different from his own. Whatever actually happened, what is certain is that Moore took on the left with as much intensity as he had taken on the Flint school board, and indeed everything else in his life until that point. This time, however, he lost, sent back to Flint with the complimentary U-Haul and the seed money for what would become his documentary, *Roger & Me*. The rematch was not long in coming.

CHAPTER FOUR

Out Like Flint

The Bunny Lady, Roger, and Me

"When *Roger & Me* came out, I would have been about ten or eleven. . . . From what I recall, it was a very hard time." These are the words of Ryan Eashoo, who was interviewed by telephone for this book. Like Michael Moore, Eashoo was born in Flint and raised in its suburb of Davison. In 1997 he graduated from Moore's own alma mater, Davison High School.

"I grew up middle class — my dad worked at the City of Flint, the Department of Public Works. They laid a lot of people off. My mom worked different secretarial jobs to make it. It was a tough time — for all Americans in the '80s, especially the early '80s, but a tough time for us in Flint. As a kid at that age, you don't really realize why things are the way they are. You don't realize that there are places that aren't so depressed. Economically. You just feel that's the norm."

Eashoo has three times nominated Moore to be inducted into their high school's hall of fame — in the five years since its inception. In January 2005, Eashoo's campaign culminated in a nationwide nomination struggle to see Moore recognized by the community. From Eashoo's own Web site, an online system of nomination was developed, allowing non-Davison residents to petition Moore's admission. Eashoo's campaign received attention in national newspapers in the U.S., Canada, and France. Although the campaign failed, Eashoo's recollection of his own formative years cuts honestly to the core of the matter: even the middle-class families of Flint were facing financial struggles. In 1980s America, two trends emerged that would shape Moore and his work: the death of local industry; and, in Michigan, the rise of the armed right wing.

The proud state was — and is — characterized by something besides its four-wheelers: the uniform of military and hunting camouflage. While activists concerned themselves with the policies of the Reagan administration on Latin America, the more insidious elements of Reaganomics were being felt in the manufacturing belt at home. With controls loosened, and labor laws rescinded, the corporate world no longer had to appease its biggest source of overhead: its workers. In the auto industry, these policies dovetailed with new competition from better foreign-made cars. By the mid '80s, factories were closing down at an unprecedented rate, and no city was hit harder than Flint. In August 1987, *Money Magazine* declared Flint the worst place to live in America, and *half* of the top ten least desirable places to have a home, "due to high crime rates, weak economies and relatively few arts and leisure activities," were in Michigan.

After any economic catastrophe, people, in desperation, will turn to voices that are strong, confident, violent, and ready to blame a visible group for their woes. This was true in 1932 Germany, and, on a much smaller scale, in 1980s America. As Michigan turned poor, it also turned violent. Coming out of Flint's '80s depression, the Flint-Decker-Detroit triangle would witness the beating of Malice Green in 1992, a Detroit black motorist who was pulled over for a traffic stop but died at the hands of two white police officers. In 1995, from Michigan's farmlands came the emergence of Timothy McVeigh, Oklahoma bomber. He had come to Decker, Michigan, just sixty-five miles outside of Flint, to be with like-minded individuals, individuals who conducted military drills in the woods in preparation for the day they might overthrow a U.S. government they saw as yielding to foreign interests, and by association, foreigners. McVeigh, along with several others, would set off a truck of explosives in front of the Oklahoma City federal building, killing 168 people. By the beginning of the new millennium, a school shooting by the youngest person ever — a Flint six-year-old — would be committed in Michigan, and documented in Moore's later film *Bowling for Columbine*. What had happened in the Great Lakes state that could lead to all this?

Before *Fahrenheit 9/11*, there was *Bowling for Columbine*; before it, there was *Roger & Me*, a documentary collaged from news footage pertaining to the economic conditions of the city of Flint — from the beehive hairdos and Pontiac parades of the 1950s, to the

fallen General Motors tower, and a rat population sur-
passing the human one in the late '80s. There was also the
film's most unforgettable sequence, a Flint woman club-
bing and butchering a rabbit (on camera), and selling its
meat for grocery money. And there was Moore's own
dogged pursuit of Roger Smith, Chairman of GM, from
whom he hoped to get answers regarding layoffs throughout the 1980s.

But even before *Roger & Me*, there was *Blood in the
Face*, a documentary initiated in the mid-'80s by New
York's Kevin Rafferty, Anne Bohlen, and James Ridgeway.
Based on Ridgeway's book of the same title, the docu-
mentary was to be a disturbing, straightforward look at
renewed Ku Klux Klan and white supremacist activity.
Not only did *Blood in the Face* show a then-nameless
movement, and escalating racism and violence in
Michigan, it was also Moore's first screen credit. Rafferty
and company knew of Moore through his work at the
Voice. Without ever having met, they phoned Moore from
New York to ask if he could get them into a Klan meeting.
Moore did. His profile appears in only one scene. By the
time *Blood in the Face* was released in 1991, Moore's familiar shape and voice would already be known for *Roger &
Me*, but working with the Rafferty crew was Moore's first
real taste of film work. He credits Rafferty (who also
directed the award-winning film, *The Atomic Café*) for
inspiration. Not only did Rafferty show Moore how to
load the film and run the sound equipment when it came
time to begin his own project, but he is also credited as
director of photography on *Roger & Me*. Later, Moore
would donate $50,000 of his *Roger & Me* earnings toward
Rafferty's next project, *Feed*.

What was Moore's role in the making of *Blood in the Face*? He flirted with one of the female supremacists and got her to talk about her hate, telling her she didn't look like "a typical Nazi," and that she looked like she could be in a Coppertone commercial. Accustomed to covering and ridiculing local neo-Nazi activity, Moore said he stepped in when the New York crew lost their nerve. According to Moore, "They didn't want to be on camera, because they thought the Klan guys might come after them. . . . So I said, 'I'll do it. I'm not worried about these guys.'"

Moore can be heard posing questions throughout, but his is not the only voice; Moore and all three producers are credited as interviewers. Very close to film's end, Moore's voice *is* clear as he argues with one of the subjects. "You will never see this day what you want to see come to be in this country . . ." he tells Alan Poe, a middle-aged Christian Identity minister who has been arguing throughout the film against the rise of black professionals, against the existence of the Holocaust, and against Jewish members of the Senate. With the exception of stark news clips of the Holocaust and the Chinese Red Army, scattered amidst footage from a neo-Nazi conference in Cohacta, Michigan, Moore's voice is the only overt opposition to the Aryan movement presented in the film. Poe begins to argue, and Moore issues the expletive "jack shit," which — though it is difficult to say with absolute certainty as their two voices merge — sounds as though it slams shut Moore's sentence, "You are not going to be able to do jack shit." Poe continues his argument, which cites God as the reason white supremacists will "win," and asks if he has found a convert, even though the answer is obviously the opposite. The screen fades to darkness.

The *Blood in the Face* documentary intensified Moore's interest in film. He had always loved movies, but the idea of making one of his own began to germinate. After his termination from *Mother Jones*, a depressed Moore began seeing films around the clock, including mainstream shoot-'em-ups in spite of his antiviolent nature. "I probably went to a movie a day," he admitted. "I would go to see everything — [Sylvester] Stallone, Arnold [Schwarzenegger], everything except ninja movies . . . and I thought 'Well, why not try and make a movie?' . . . It didn't look that hard. Most of 'em are pretty lousy. I didn't know what I'd do it on. . . ."

Upon his return to Flint, post–*Mother Jones*, post–Ralph Nader, Moore was, for the first time in his adult life, without a political or creative forum for expression. An unfortunate set of events lent Moore the ambition and the forum he so needed. It was November 6, 1986, 5:37 p.m. when the story appeared on CBS news. Roger Smith, Chairman of General Motors, made a statement: "Today we're announcing the closing of eleven of our older plants." Moore had found his movie. Only two years earlier, in 1984, the company had handed out $322 million in profit share to 530,000 employees in the U.S. GM and the United Auto Workers had also signed a three-year labor agreement offering unprecedented income security for employees. Moore's reaction to the closings: "The hell with this. I gotta do something about it. . . ."

The Nader organization, however, disputed the idea that the film was Moore's idea. Said Nader associate James Musselman, also a Philadelphia lawyer: "*Roger & Me* glorifies Mr. Moore's role while forgetting about all the middle-of-the-road people who worked so hard on these issues and don't get any credit." More irksome to Nader himself was that Moore did not complete the work for the Nader organization that he had been paid to do. Some overlap existed between Moore's tenure with the *Moore Weekly* newsletter to which Nader had assigned him and Moore's commencing of the project *Roger & Me*, which wound up being given precedence. Nader claimed Moore had been paid for writing he never completed, and Musselman added that Moore drew *Roger & Me* information and inspiration from Nader's own General Motors–focused book *The Big Boys*, which prominently profiled Roger Smith. Only a month prior, newspaper articles acknowledged that Nader had "donated office space and a little seed money to go after his old adversary, GM."

The end credits of Moore's film acknowledge Nader as well, but obviously the two men disagreed on the terms of whatever money passed between them. If the money were paid back, Nader stated it would be put into a journalistic nonprofit group known as Essential One. Anyone who has followed Moore's career knows that relations between Nader and himself have, over the years, gone back and forth from friendly to chilly to unabashedly rude — on both sides. However, Moore would go on to work with Nader again in the 2000 Presidential campaign.

As to the actual making of *Roger & Me*, Moore may not have known much about film, but he was already familiar with GM and the company's politics, pre-Nader. Working for the *Voice* hadn't earned him staying power at *Mother Jones*, but it did give him a leg up when it came to reporting on local corporations. Shooting for *Roger & Me* began only three months after Roger Smith's announcement. Moore's camera began rolling on February 11, 1987, and filming wouldn't be completed for another two and a half years.

Moore's settlement with *Mother Jones* would not come through until 1989, when the parties arrived at an out-of-court agreement. In the meantime, Moore and his partner and now coproducer Glynn drew on earlier fundraising skills, and were able to organize a Tuesday night bingo, with the film as their own charity. Moore sold his house and held two garage sales. They solicited funds where they could, including from actor Ed Asner, of *Mary Tyler Moore Show* fame, but also from the bank of Mom and Dad: Michael's own parents. The film itself would cost $160,000. At $400 per roll for film stock, Moore and his crew shot sparingly.

At the same time, they knew to keep the camera rolling — even when their subjects (often amused receptionists, disgruntled security guards, and by-the-book P.R. managers) thought it had been shut off. Moore would be critiqued for this by journalists who felt he used — and still uses — the working class for a laugh, since middle-class people are less likely to work the retail counters of large corporations, or to work in security, even for the most posh of country clubs.

One such critic was Harlan Jacobson, who profiled Moore in *Film Comment*, one of his first major interviews for *Roger & Me*. Another would be Pauline Kael, writing for the *New Yorker*. "The picture is like the work of a slick ad exec," she writes in her review. "It does something that is humanly very offensive: *Roger & Me* uses its leftism as a superior attitude. Members of the audience can laugh at ordinary working people and still feel that they're taking a politically correct position." Another interviewer — Spencer Rumsey from *Newsday* — described a scene in which a San Francisco waitress offers a seemingly endless list of different kinds of coffee drinks: "It drew a big laugh from the audience when I saw it. Weren't we laughing at her expense?"

Moore countered, "The people in Detroit are not laughing at that waitress. They have nothing against that waitress. It's everything that that represents. We go into a restaurant in Detroit, we have one choice. Maybe two. But wealth has all of these choices."

Perspective was everything. Wealthy viewers may have been laughing at the waitress; less wealthy viewers were laughing with her — at the tedium of her job, to which they could likely relate.

But before examining criticisms of *Roger & Me*, we should examine the film frame by frame, regardless of the number of times we have seen it. *Roger & Me*, in retrospect, is a very different film than it was in its day. As an audience, we now also have a political perspective of the time period we could not have had in 1989. We also know now that it marks an incredible shift in the documentary form. *Roger & Me* established the methods for which Moore would become famous in the ensuing decade.

Moore's hope was to actually convince Roger Smith to spend a day riding around the town of Flint in a van with the film crew so that Smith could see for himself the devastation that had been wreaked upon the people there by the GM plant closings. "It was gonna be like *My Dinner With André* on wheels. . . . But of course that didn't happen," Moore said in interview, referencing Louis Malle's popular 1981 art house movie that used only one location and a long conversation. What did happen was that Moore pursued "Roger" at GM headquarters, shareholders' meetings, Michigan social clubs, and even a New

York hotel, hoping to corner him, and force his invitation upon Smith personally. Moore honestly believed that at some point during the two and a half years of shooting, Smith would relent, or at the very least, allow Moore an interview. However, the 14th floor of GM headquarters, where Smith's office was located, continued to elude Moore's film crew, with each effort raising the level of filmic comedy — and civil frustration.

Though critics would argue the veracity of the facts used in the film, *Roger & Me* was one of the first documentaries to exploit comedy in an otherwise serious genre. "How would you describe Charlie Chaplin?" Moore asked of one of his interviewers in 1989. "Great film comedian, right? Yeah. But no. His films are all tragedies. He was being abused by the state, thrown in jail, kicked out of his job, losing the girl, riding off into the sunset with nothing. That's not how we remember him, though. We remember the comedy. He used humor as a weapon."

According to Moore, the techniques used in the film were, at first, largely accidental. He kept walking amateurishly into frame, but then found the people he was interviewing tended to relax more when he allowed himself to be filmed alongside them. In retrospect, the title *Roger & Me* is perfectly suited to the film: it allows that there be some "me" in the movie, a bumbling personality for the story to revolve around. Indeed, with this device, Moore softens the political nature of the film. He is able instead to force it to adhere to the comedic form, providing a story arc. From the film's very first shot, Moore's story arc focuses on Moore himself. We see a small child wearing a Popeye mask, clowning.

Looking at film styles, documentary and propaganda are thought to be mutually exclusive cousins that never kiss. On the one side there are the *Why We Fight* films, made during WWII by the conscripted Frank Capra (who, when left to his own devices, was more likely to direct fictional pictures like *It's A Wonderful Life*). With bold editing and witty, sharp voice-over, *Why We Fight* could never be mistaken for anything but a spirit-rouser. On the other side, there is the very first documentary feature, 1922's *Nanook of the North*. Plain, with simple edits, we would never take it for more than a snapshot of Inuit life. In hindsight, we now know that much of *Nanook* was staged, and that Capra's films, which mix newsreel and action movie footage, presaged the dominant documentary style of the 1990s.

For the method of *Roger & Me*, Moore did learn many lessons from Rafferty, whose previous documentary, *The Atomic Café*, was the first popular film to use stock and educational footage edited at breakneck speed for black humor and grim comment. As well, Moore was taking notice of the other growing trend of documentary cinema in the '80s, typified by German filmmaker Werner Herzog and his American student, Errol Morris. This could be called "the documentary of the outsider." Its concerns are marginalized figures, not history-makers and heroes: the grieving pet owners in Morris's *Gates of Heaven*, or the blind and deaf in Herzog's *Land of Silence and Darkness*. The outsider documentary was a humanist movement that, like Moore's inclusion of the Bunny Lady in *Roger & Me*, would sometimes be misinterpreted as exploitive. In Moore's satire, the antihero characters become the story's only tellers, sharply contrasting the wealthy targets of the film — like Roger Smith — whose dialogue is conspicuously absent. Perhaps these stand-in players tell it too well for some people's tastes.

With Smith missing from much of the movie — seen only from a distance or in news clips — his double becomes Deputy Fred Ross. The kindhearted evictor, with his just-doing-my-job casualness, further devastates Flint, but because (unlike Smith) he is obviously also a member of the community, Ross has to make peace with the blood on his hands. Ross appears after every failed attempt of Moore's to contact the CEO. At the film's devastating climax, Smith and Ross are intercut: Smith reads *A Christmas Carol* at the GM holiday party, while Ross carries a family's tinseled tree to the curb.

The unique element added to the film's mix was Moore himself. From the opening frame of him as a child, and his personal voice-over, we know what we are going to watch is a subjective satire. In *Roger & Me*, Moore's hit-and-run interview style also developed, and, as Roger Ebert pointed out, served as an important technique for getting a point across to the viewer. Moore is an experienced journalist who knows that he will never get an interview with Smith in the manner he adopts throughout the film. But by approaching CEOs in the style any audience member might use — by going to the front door — he becomes again, that Everyman mirror.

Audiences would respond to the Everyman from the film's first showing, appropriately enough, over Labor Day weekend at the Telluride Festival in Colorado. The screening would be emblematic of good things to come for *Roger & Me*. "I remember [Bill and Stella Pence] telling me that they had added more screenings of *Roger & Me* than they had added for any other film in the history of the festival," Moore has said, but he almost didn't have the film ready in time for this festival, where Gene Siskel (and Warner Bros.) would first view it. Though Du Art, Moore's New York film lab, had given him a generous price break, the sound for the film would still cost approximately $12,000, and Moore "didn't have a dime left." After viewing the film, Bill Nickelson, Du Art's manager, agreed to do the sound for free, saying Moore could pay for it later, if he ever made money from it. The film fared well at its first festival — so well that Moore received more than one generous distribution offer. Years later, Moore said that without the *pro bono* sound mix, he never would have made it to his first festival. Without that first festival, Warner Bros. might never have seen it. "It all came by that act of generosity. . . . So I've always gone back there with my other films. . . . When you get those breaks in life, you never want to forget that."

Everything was up and running after that for Moore, who was stunned by the whole experience. "You have to understand that we had been working on the film for over three years, we had no money, we only got to Telluride because they flew us there," Moore said two years later in an interview with the Telluride Film Festival's Geoff Hanson. According to Moore, he and Glynn had left the New York lab at three in the morning. To get to Telluride, they boarded a 7 a.m. flight from La Guardia, without having seen the final print of the film. The first time they viewed it was on the Mason's Cinema screen in Telluride.

"It was one of those moments I'll never forget," said Moore. "People started laughing during the titles, and it was then that we thought we might have pulled it off. . . ."

From that moment on, Moore said, "we really didn't get back home for more than a day at a time for the next eleven months. There were all the things in dealing with Warner Brothers. Then we went on a huge promotional tour in which we visited 110 cities."

Warner Bros. offered $3 million and blasted *Roger & Me* into 1300 theaters, including small towns, after initially agreeing to put it in 800. It was this commitment to having the film show in front of as many audiences as possible that enticed Moore into the agreement. Universal and Miramax were both promising studios at the time, and weighed in with strong bids, but Warner Bros. won Moore over by agreeing to some of his nonmonetary demands. In addition to raising the number of theaters the film would show in, Warner Bros. agreed to pay housing for two years for the evicted families depicted in the film. They also arranged an abundant number of free tickets for those showing unemployment cards at theaters, and $250,000 to pay for Moore and his Flint associates to complete Moore's original goal: a tour to community halls and churches in other economically depressed cities, where the film would be shown for free. Moore stood on the lawn of the Genessee County Jail in Flint to sign the Warner Bros. contract. The jail is featured prominently in the film, as Moore interviews a GM-worker-turned-prison-guard about Flint's soaring crime rate in the wake of the plant closures.

The official movie release was December 22, 1989 — and *Roger & Me*, a film about corporate negligence, was, surprisingly, billed as the feel-good film of the holiday season. Even more surprising was that, in spite of its grim messages, the film lived up to those expectations. Because all movie theaters in Flint had closed, the world premiere for *Roger & Me* was held at Showcase Cinemas in the satellite town of Burton, Michigan. But there was also a New York premiere, complete with an after-party including a put-on working class spread of franks and beans.

"I had this dream," Moore told D.D. Guttenplan of *Newsday* the week of the film's official release. "The revolution started and there I was in this limo. I was banging on the windows, screaming 'No! No! Warners made me ride this.' So I made them take back the limo." It was no wonder Moore was bounding around his hotel room, nervously jabbering at journalists about his dreams. *Roger & Me* had already made *Rolling Stone*'s Ten Best list — weeks before the movie released in front of mainstream audiences. Anticipation, joy, and fear were all palpable.

The other shoe would drop, of course. The November/December issue of *Film Comment* featured an interview with Moore wherein Harlan Jacobson took him to task for the sequence of events in *Roger & Me*. "Motor Mouth Michael Moore" adorned the cover — covered in tire treads that certainly hadn't been part of the promotional image. The director had been run over, philosophically. Jacobson critiqued the liberties Moore took with his presentation. The facts and footage contained in *Roger & Me* span a decade. Layoffs occurred throughout the 1980s in Flint, but the plant closures are cited specifically in the news clip (from November 1986) that inspired the film's production.

To an audience approaching the film as a straightforward documentary, it seems like absolute lunacy that a prosperous city could lose its entire economy and its social systems between the 1986 announcements of plant closures and the film's release in late 1989. In reality, by the time Moore started his film, Flint was already on its way down. The GM plant closures in Michigan were just the final nail in the coffin. Moore chronicles the whole decade, beginning with Reagan's visit to Flint to take some unemployed auto workers out for pizza during his first presidential bid. Critics argued that because Reagan was president for two terms, viewers are likely to assume this occurred in 1986 or '87. But an observant viewer should be able to tell, not only by the clothing and hairstyles of the subjects, but by the difference in film quality, that this footage was neither taken at the same time as the rest, nor by the same film crew. Articles following on Jacobson's would debate when the cash register was stolen from the pizza parlor. In voice-over, Moore-the-narrator jokes that this was the only good thing to come out of the Reagan lunch — that at least it was profitable for somebody. The cash register apparently actually went missing in the commotion of the preparation two days before Reagan's arrival.

Then there were the preposterous tactics Flint city officials used to try to attract tourism to the city: the construction of a posh Hyatt-Regency, and — everyone's favorite — AutoWorld, an indoor theme park dedicated to local history. But these two white elephants were actually built in 1982 and 1984; they were not responses to the 1987 closures, but to an already-tanking economy. Such shortsighted investments sank the town further into debt just before NAFTA was ratified and GM moved its productions south, essentially closing down the city that it had built. Defending his film in *Newsday*, Moore said, "It's only a few people who don't want to deal with the politics in the movie who are saying that. All the facts in the movie are true. All the context is true. They're only accusing me of being a journalist — attempting to tell a story with fifty hours of film footage edited to an hour and a half."

Following closely on the *Film Comment* piece, Pauline Kael of the *New Yorker* rallied against *Roger & Me*, using Jacobson's facts as her own coupled with a deeper bite. Calling Moore "a big, shambling joker in windbreaker and baseball cap," Kael accused him of using people as filler. "He asks them broad questions about the high rate of unemployment and the soaring crime rate, and their responses make them look like phonies or stupes. . . ." wrote Kael. "I had stopped believing what Moore was saying very early; he was just too glib. Later, when he told us about the tourist schemes, I began to feel I was watching a film version of the thirties bestseller *A Short Introduction to the History of Human Stupidity.* . . ."

Kael, like Jacobson and others to come, also took issue with the number of plant closings. There were eleven in total, but nowhere in the film does Moore say or imply that all of these plants were located in Flint — the news footage clearly states that Flint would simply be the most affected by the closures. Of course, Kael may not have been able to double-check the film's actual content, as Moore refused to send it to the well-known film reviewer, insisting instead that she make the trip to the theater in New York to view it.

Years ago on his Weblog, Moore detailed a very funny story about how, shortly after the release of *Roger & Me*, he began to think of himself as an "artiste." When the studio called him to ask if they could send a videotape to Kael for review, Moore's reply was that he hadn't made a video, he'd made a movie, meant to be viewed on the large screen. He claimed not to know who Kael was, even though her reputation was such that this was unlikely. He also claimed he had never read the *New Yorker*, something which for a journalist and ex–*Mother Jones* editor was even more unlikely. Moore's Web diary over the years has often flipped back and forth in this manner, volleying between so-glib-it-must-be-self-parody and the absolute earnestness of his tirades. Does he really believe that if he had mailed Kael the videotape she would have been persuaded to like his movie? Or is he just being the comedian that is his nature?

"Oh brother. What an idiot . . ." Moore wrote of himself in his ten-year retrospective on the Kael/*New Yorker* incident: "They called Ms. Kael and told her my response. She was elderly and it was winter and she lived over 150 miles away. And I, the great film auteur Michael Moore, was demanding she drive down to New York City to view my masterpiece." Kael did exactly that. The next day at the annual meeting of the New York Film Critics, Kael "wasted" *Roger & Me*, voicing her opposition to the film while critics were preparing to vote on the organization's best film of the year.

In spite of Kael's objections, *Roger & Me* did win the New York Film Critics Circle Awards. Roger Ebert and Gene Siskel were perhaps Moore's greatest defenders — better than he could ever be for himself, as Moore has always tended to react to criticism, when it would be wiser to simply bite his tongue. Ebert championed the film after seeing it at Telluride, but Siskel quickly followed in his praise of it. It was Siskel who arranged to film Moore, Ebert, and himself on the hood of a Cadillac at a

GM dealership in Chicago — with no protest from the dealer. At year's end, Ebert placed *Roger & Me* at No. 5 on his "10 Best Films" list; Siskel one-upped him and placed it at No. 2. After Kael's assault on the film, Ebert responded in the *Chicago Sun Times* by saying that Kael and Jacobson, with their factual complaints, had both missed the point entirely. Ebert wrote that he had responded to the film immediately for a variety of reasons, including its humor, its anger, its ability to consistently entertain, and because "it said things that had not been said in the movies in a long time: that the MBA-powered 'success ethic' is just another word for greed, and that beneath their benign P.R.-powered images, big corporations are as ruthless as they ever were."

Ebert agreed with Kael that Moore was glib, but felt that was the obvious intention. "He was thumbing his nose at GM," Ebert wrote, "he was taking cheap shots, he knew it, we knew it, and it was about time."

Ebert went on to say that the manipulation of fact to suit Moore's thesis was obvious, and implied that anyone who cared about that manipulation was missing a point satirists and ironists had been making for generations. "What *Roger & Me* supplies about General Motors, Flint, and big corporations," Ebert wrote, "is both more important and more rare than facts. It supplies poetry, a viewpoint, indignation, opinion, anger, and humor."

At the Sundance Festival in Utah, Ebert spoke to other artistic filmmakers of the day. All of them agreed that there could be no interesting documentary form without editing or manipulation. "What you do on a documentary is, you get the best footage you can, and put it together to make the best point you can," said Ed Lachman, a cinematographer who had worked with Herzog. Lachman continued, "If everything had to be in chronological order, there aren't many documentaries that could pass the test." Karen Thorson, before directing her own films, worked for many years with Albert Maysles (inventor of the unobtrusive style of documentary, or *cinema verité*, and best known for *Salesman* and *Gimme Shelter*). Regarding the criticisms leveled at *Roger & Me*, her response to Ebert was, "Are the critics of this movie seeing a documentary for the first time? Can't they tell by the tone what the movie is doing?"

In the *New York Times*, Richard Bernstein called *Roger & Me* "a kind of David and Goliath revenge story, in which a modest, plain-speaking nobody triumphs morally over an evil corporate giant." Bernstein pointed out that the complaints raised by Jacobson and Kael were based on the assumption that "a documentary is a piece of filmed journalism, and that it should obey the same rules of balance and objectivity that newspapers and television news are supposed to obey." As a satire, Bernstein asked, wasn't it necessary for *Roger & Me* to rely on exaggeration? Bernstein's article, from February 1990, suggested it was possible to take a middle position on the film: that as a satire, *Roger & Me* did not need to adhere strictly to the timeline of events or to "unbiased presentation of data," but that certainly some of the film's impact was lessened by the unreliability of its narrator. Comparing *Roger & Me* to Jonathan Swift's "A Modest Proposal" (in which Swift wryly suggested the Irish famine would be solved by the parents eating their young), Bernstein argued that the audience ought to be fully aware of Moore's tongue-in-cheek tone. He also pointed out the purpose of these tactics: that such parodies often draw greater attention to social problems than standard journalism. "If, for example," wrote Bernstein, "Mr. Moore had entitled his film something like *General Motors and Flint: The Making of a Calamity*, he would have been signaling a conventional journalistic treatment. To his supporters, the title *Roger & Me* clearly shows in advance that irreverence, eccentricity, and a highly personalized view are all among his primary intentions."

Unfortunately, the damage had already been done. *Roger & Me* was shut out of Academy Award nominations; Moore would wait more than twelve years before he would finally stand in front of the Academy.

Film critics were not the only ones offended by *Roger & Me*. Flint attorney (and now judge) Larry Stecco sued Moore and Warner Bros. for defamation under "false light invasion of privacy," and won. Stecco was an active Democrat, and had defended Moore back in the days when the school board was attempting to give him the slip by arranging meetings without him. But Stecco felt Moore's portrayal of him at the Flint annual Great Gatsby party made him look foolish. Modeled after the F. Scott Fitzgerald novel of roaring '20s opulence before the looming crash, an expansive green lawn is lined with white linen tables laden with food and drink. Endless trays of shrimp are adorned by glass swans and fresh flower arrangements. Milling about are well-dressed men and women, and several out-of-work actors (notably black) who will serve for the afternoon as live statuary in period costume. On camera, the tuxedoed Stecco comments that the people who are laid off are facing hard times, but that others are still working.

Moore asks him what the good aspects of Flint are. A woman prompts Stecco referring to his children and ballet. Pressed, he says, "Ballet, hockey. It's a great place to live." Though Stecco's comments are innocent enough, the film's next shot shows an intrusive eviction by Deputy Ross as he enters an empty residence and puts to the curb a family's belongings, including close-shots of bedroom furnishings belonging to two children. The finished film, plus unused footage, was viewed by an eight-person jury and Genesee County Circuit Judge Judith Fullerton, who decided in Stecco's favor, awarding him $6250.

Stecco was not the only person in *Roger & Me* unhappy with his portrayal. Another was Bob Eubanks, successful son of Flint and host of TV's *The Newlywed Game*. Moore interviewed him as he prepared to host a stage version of the game show in downtown Flint. Eubanks is quite relaxed in front of the camera before going onstage. He protests Moore's use of the word "breasts," saying he would never use this word in his game show. He then goes on to tell a graphic joke involving Jewish women and AIDS. According to Moore, when the film came out, Eubanks joined the Anti-Defamation League of Southern California on television in protesting the film as anti-Semitic. Warner Bros. refused to censor the offending line.

Years later, it is fascinating to see the hubbub caused by a novice filmmaker taking on not the giant of a country — as Moore would later — but a corporation. *Roger & Me*'s harshest critics, Kael and Jacobson, were correct in their opinions that the time line of the film was skewed, and that the story was one-sided. Moore ignored facts that did not suit him, such as the number of employees still working in Flint in 1989 under GM. However, time would prove Moore — and *Roger & Me* — right. As of 2002, there were still five GM plants open, but according to the company itself, there were only 15,200 GM employees in Genesse County, down from 82,000 in 1970. On July 23, 2002, the *Detroit News* Autos Insider section reported: "One of eight homes in Flint is vacant, the largest percentage in the state, according to the latest U.S. Census." The report went on to alert the public: "The city, strapped for cash, cut back on maintenance of parks and other city sites. It also closed the city jail last year and ended the city ambulance service. It has closed a police precinct and a fire station." Though there are still some successful commercial areas in Flint, a beautiful library and museums, the city has certainly seen its share of slums and closed storefronts — and continues to do so.

Moore has said that one of the most painful things about making *Roger & Me* was that it didn't "save" his hometown. In the 2003 commentary for *Roger & Me*, Moore acknowledged a personal sense of failure. He admitted that perhaps it was a crazy idea, that he and Glynn had set their goals too high, believing a film could save a town. To this day, critics still accuse Moore of living in the past, insisting things have changed in Michigan economically. Things have. Certain areas in Michigan have swelled with affluence. Others, like Flint, have declined. Moore wrote in 2000, "As bad as it may get, the head of General Motors still has the same number of votes as you or I — one! And there's more of us than there are of him. Never forget that."

Flint wasn't saved, but *Roger & Me* did get people talking — and talking, and talking, and talking. A provocative piece, it grossed almost $8 million in theaters worldwide, and led to a plethora of straightforward journalistic pieces on General Motors and other corporations' policies toward workers.

In Flint these days, there is still hope, and even a few crazy ideas still flying around. Ryan Eashoo had one himself: honor Moore at home, in the Davison High School Hall of Fame. Said Eashoo, "I just believe in what he does. I don't agree with him all the time, but I believe he's very talented. I believe he speaks for people who don't really have a voice.... It started off just me and then I told some friends over drinks in Flint. I said, 'Hey, c'mon, we need to do this. Michael deserves this.'" As part of his campaign, Eashoo set up a Web site and began receiving sixty to seventy E-mails per day from people all over the country who wanted to share their opinions — positive or negative — about Moore. All of it fascinates Eashoo, who believes the communities of Flint and Davison support Moore for the most part. "The reaction is mixed," Eashoo says. "It's about 75% supportive and about 25% opposed, that I've talked to."

According to Eashoo, who by day, works in real estate sales, "the problem that people in Flint have is, when Michael Moore did the film *Roger & Me*, [they] thought that he was taking a stab at Flint. And in reality — in my opinion — Michael Moore said, 'Hey, wake up. This is what this corporation has done to this town. This town and the people in this town. They built General Motors: the people that were born here, the people that moved here, the people that generation after generation worked in the factories, and all the tax breaks that the city has given this corporation allowed it to become one of the biggest corporations in the world.' And a lot of people

EMILY SCHULTZ

don't realize, Michael Moore didn't go out to make a film. When he made *Roger & Me*, all he was doing was trying to make a film piece that he could take into union halls. . . . He wasn't making a film to make money and make people look bad and to become a bestseller or the best documentary ever."

Moore did take his film into union halls. He donated substantial earnings from the film back to the city of Flint, and also established a supportive organization for independent filmmakers. He didn't save the town, but he succeeded at what he set out to do — he drew the public's attention to the issue of how big business operates, and how it would continue to operate under the North American Free Trade Agreement. He made a mainstream documentary, a documentary watched by working people across the country, and across the world. It would not be long before Moore's work would be seen by hundreds of thousands more — as he moved accidentally from film to that forum known as the "idiot box," with one of the smartest, most aggressive shows ever to grace the small screen: a kind of lefty *That's Incredible!* known as *TV Nation*.

CHAPTER FIVE

So Long AutoWorld,

Hello *TV Nation*

When the first season of *TV Nation* aired in, I think 1993 or '94, I was completely blown away. It incorporated all the things I had wanted to do, combining comedy and journalism and political activism. And there was a wonderfully reckless, "I can't believe they got this on TV" feel to it.

— *John Derevlany, writer and performer for* TV Nation

Without a doubt, if the name "Crackers" is mentioned in front of *TV Nation* fans, their eyes will go misty and they will begin to chuckle. The mere summoning of a mental image of this fictional superhero — a seven-foot-tall chicken-with-a-mission (to bust businessmen and businesswomen for their misdeeds) — is the equivalent of placing a puppy in the lap of any conversation. The unanimous response is a reverent and dewy, "Awww!" At least, such was the reaction whenever I told friends or contemporaries I was engaging in correspondence with John Derevlany, a *TV Nation* writer, and the man inside the mythical bird suit, a.k.a. Crackers the Corporate Crime-Fighting Chicken.

Who was this Crackers character? And why is this "corporate crime-fighter" so emblematic of Michael Moore's *TV Nation* years? According to Moore, and producer and partner Kathleen Glynn, "Each year in America, we lose $4 billion to burglary and robbery, but we lose $200 billion due to corporate fraud. And each year, forty-five thousand more people lose their lives due to corporate workplace hazards than those who are murdered by handguns." This grim statistic surely can't conjure the gentle awe described above, yet it is directly responsible for the creation of the Crackers persona.

"The original concept was that Crackers would be just a 'mascot,'" said Derevlany in my interview with him. "Someone who would stand around and look funny, comic relief as we did otherwise dry, nonvisual stories on fraud, corruption, pollution, etc. I still think it's a brilliant idea." The idea of "corporate crime" was one that Moore had worked with before — while running the *Voice*. But this time the idea would come to life in three-dimensional full feathered glory. And Moore's team understood why. According to Derevlany, "The reason these important, billion-dollar stories don't receive the kind of attention they merit is because they're just not visual enough for

EMILY SCHULTZ

TV. Sure, companies like Enron have raped us for billions, but where's the excitement? The blood on the pavement? The police chase? It's just a boring story. That's partly where Crackers came in."

In 1985, Roger Kerson penned an article in Moore's newspaper the *Michigan Voice*: "Crime in the Suites: Michigan's Corporate Crooks and Big Business Bullies." It examined the role of the Ford Motor Company in the deadly Pinto scandal. But in 1993, the idea for a mascot who would fight corporate wrongdoing was Moore's, based on the existing character of McGruff the Crime Dog, whose television presence amounted to commercials that gave tips on good citizenship and recognizing street crime in one's neighborhood. Moore was actually obsessed with the little crime dog, who encouraged the American public to "Help take a bite out of crime!" He intended to expand this idea for *TV Nation*. Moore developed the concept with writer Jay Martel, who pitched the idea of a crime-fighting canary. According to Derevlany, "Michael changes it to chicken, because, as he explained, 'Chickens are funny.'"

Crackers was born as little more than a rough pen-doodle: an enormous bird in a hat and tie with a bold "C" emblazoned upon his chickeny chest. This logo would later be replaced by the *TV Nation* emblem. Crackers soon evolved into a masked capon crusader not so distant in stature from other beloved television figures such as *Sesame Street*'s Big Bird or *Looney Tunes*' blowhard cartoon rooster, Foghorn Leghorn. Crackers' purpose, however, was far more adult. As Crackers grew — into a three-dimensional chicken suit later inhabited by Derevlany — so did his mission. He would chase after the advertisers of the very TV show he was to appear on, and take corporations to task for their lack of responsibility to citizens and country. Introduced as a regular cast member for segments in Moore's '90s newsmagazine show *TV Nation*, Crackers charged in whenever the series' human crew found themselves afraid the content would be too financially dangerous for the network to continue to support. For example, Crackers attempted to pin the term "extortion" on banks, such as Boston Corp., which was demanding tax breaks from the city of New York; stormed to the rescue in Philadelphia over CoreStates Banks' outrageous $25 fee per bounced check — actually inspiring State Representative Babette Josephs to introduce a bill in the Pennsylvania legislature limiting bounced check fees to a more reasonable $7.50; and personally gathered lab samples on behalf of citizens in St. Louis with environmental concerns pertaining to the Doe Run lead foundry. Once, without thought of personal safety, Crackers, on a search for answers for striking newspaper workers, rushed the *Detroit Free Press* building — resulting in his being thrown ten feet by irate security, and necessitating a trip to the hospital for the not-so-chicken chicken. Not only did these kinds of stunts make Crackers famous, they exemplify the audacity of the *TV Nation* show as a whole.

An hour-long weekly program adding humor to the newsmagazine formula of *60 Minutes*, *TV Nation* went one step further than its competition: it was not objective at all, and completely upfront about its agenda. "Correspondents" such as lefty comedian Janeane Garofalo, MTV's Karen Duffy, and even Moore's old *Voice* auto worker columnist Ben Hamper, reported on a range of bizarre and emblematic American phenomenon, such as prisons as a growth industry, the racism of cabbies, or the number of pets prescribed Prozac by veterinarians. These correspondents often led crusades to change the policies of institutions or communities — as when Garofalo carried out a Beach Party invasion, rounding up a troop to take by storm the purportedly "private" beach of an all-rich, all-white community in Greenwich, Connecticut, and force them to share.

Political alliances and moral decisions were obvious. The show was also forthrightly ridiculous, kicking off with opening music meant to invoke "Metallica and the *Leave It to Beaver* theme song," and including in the regular lineup several professional statistical polls of the American public conducted by a Midwestern company. Widgery and Associates was paid by the network to support *Saturday Night Live*–style answers including, "45% of Americans believe that if space aliens could pick up C-SPAN and see Sonny Bono speaking on the floor of Congress, they would never visit the Earth," and "16% of Perot voters believe if dolphins were really smart, they could get out of those nets."

"I like to think of *TV Nation* as the anti-TV magazine show, breaking the rules of TV," said Moore at the time. Correspondent Duffy seconded this statement in an interview with Moore, her then-boss, referring to the popular conception of him as a "world-class smart-ass with solid-gold cojones."

How did the man from Flint make the jump from the 110-city grassroots-doc road show to meeting with Hollywood execs to discuss his very own TV show? He did what many people do after a major success — he failed. Along the road in Moore's attempt to make another feature film, television appeared like some kind of natural disaster that had been thrown across his path. At least, that's how he tells it in his book *Adventures in a TV Nation*, a television-years memoir, coauthored with Glynn.

Moore's life, post–*Roger & Me*, was a whirlwind of interviews and media battles. From the denouncement of the film's "documentary" status by Pauline Kael, to opposition from Ralph Nader, the United Auto Workers Union, and General Motors (who, Moore claimed, sent out "truth packages" to media networks highlighting what they saw as the falsities in his film), to appearances on the *Tonight Show*, and *The Larry King Show*, Moore had his work cut out for him. Though he had done promotional work for both the *Voice* and *Mother Jones*, *Roger & Me* was promoted on an entirely different scale. Suddenly he was in front of everyone else's cameras. As he wrote in July 1990 in the *New York Times*: "Twenty times a day I answered the same thirty questions. To keep myself from sinking into some catatonic state of boredom, I began to make up new answers to the questions and change them every day." Moore joked, "I believe that on only three occasions I was asked something different. 'How old were you when you lost your virginity?' (*People* magazine), 'Do you believe in God?' (*The Chicago Tribune*), and 'Will you sign an autograph for my poodle?' (*The New Yorker*)"

There was also the harrying experience of going home. In turns loved, honored, fed scores more heartbreaking layoff stories, cold-shouldered, and harassed, Moore learned that home is not always a comfortable place. The town played a tug-of-war with Moore and where it stood on the film. He was invited to sign copies of the vhs release of *Roger & Me* at a local video store to a turnout of several hundred, then he was prohibited from appearing on certain radio and television stations in the area. Talk show host Phil Donahue made the trip to Flint to broadcast on the city's reaction to the movie. According to Moore, Flint police intervened ten minutes before taping to inform Moore of a possible sniper situation, and to offer him a bulletproof vest. In the year following *Roger & Me*, Moore had done more traveling than he ever had in his life. To believe that he could be the same person he was before *Roger & Me* was both foolish and wishful, in spite of his continued insistence that he still owned only "three pairs of blue jeans and one Detroit Tigers cap."

The spirit of a man may not change, but his circumstances and outlook do. As he told *Esquire* magazine in 1993, "I was shopping in Flint, and one of the employees got on the phone: 'Attention, Kmart shoppers. Michael Moore has entered the store.' Know what I'm saying? And I'm hiding, you know, behind the Valvoline."

Of course, Moore had been drawing attention to himself his whole life. From his grade school newspaper projects, to his pranks during choir performances, to his career as a local politician, to newspaper publisher, to Michael Moore the documentary filmmaker. The question was, if not a life of luxury doing little but lounging and Kmart shopping, what next? The answer was not television, but a feature fictional film. During this time, Moore was being invited to premieres. He was sitting on panels, and giving instruction to other aspiring filmmakers. Moore pulled out his checkbook at an Independent Film Project conference in New York, and started a new form of instant granting. The Center for Alternative Media was not a typical foundation, as Moore readily admitted in an interview with *People's Weekly World*. "It's kind of like I see something and I just call up the person and say, 'What's your address? I want to send you a check. It's really more from me, keeping with the spirit of *Roger & Me*." The incredible irony, he explained, was that he received the money from Time Warner and was able to "recycle it into anticorporate areas."

In the end, Moore gave away 50% of the earnings from *Roger & Me* — $400,000 donated in grants to filmmakers whom he selected because he personally liked their work. Moore helped to fund the film *Just Another Girl On the IRT*, by Leslie Harris, a black filmmaker, because he found it "appalling that we're in the 100th year of cinema, and there has never been in the U.S. a film directed by an African American woman, and released by Hollywood. . . ." But for all Moore's charity, he was torn between the world of film and the world of Flint. In the devastated city in 1990, there were many worthy causes, but Moore was one of the only filmmakers. And with his sudden emergence in the world of film, it was logical that he should continue making films rather than camping out as the returned hometown boy, part defender, part desperado.

At the Sundance Festival in 1991, just days after the Gulf War began, Moore found the seed of the idea he believed would be his next project, a screenplay he would write himself and call *Canadian Bacon*. Curiously, the incident of inspiration would echo a more recent media event.

"The bombing had started in Iraq, and four days later we were at the Sundance Film Festival and I really thought that as independent filmmakers we should take a stand against this war," Moore recalled in the *People's Weekly World*. He approached John Sayles, the closing night emcee, and asked if he minded presenting a statement — according to Moore, "this resolution that we could vote on. It said something simple like, 'We group of independent filmmakers oppose the American war in Iraq.' John said, 'Yeah, it's a great idea.'" When Sayles began to read it, people began "hissing and booing him down, yelling 'This isn't politics, this is a film festival, hand out the awards.'" Moore expounded, "Now this was a group of independent filmmakers, not ditto heads, people that you think are of like mind. I was shocked. I came home thinking, if this group of people has fallen for the support of the Gulf War, my work is cut out for me."

With this reaction as early as 1991 to political speeches at film awards ceremonies, it is obvious Moore knew the reaction he would get long before he took the stage years later to accept his Oscar for *Bowling for Columbine*. Yet in 2003, he would speak of "fictitious presidents" and "fictitious wars" anyway — and to a much more mainstream crowd. Moore would lecture on the Iraq war, to him so much an echo of the Gulf War. "Shame on you, Mr. Bush," he would declare from the awards podium. Did he expect America had changed substantially in the intervening twelve years? Could it be he was a man intent on saying something important — something moral — knowing full well from past experience what the reaction and the consequences would be?

Regardless, Moore's *Canadian Bacon* would begin from this moment at Sundance, George Bush Sr.'s Operation Desert Storm raging overseas. Without *Canadian Bacon* — years in development, meeting with Hollywood producers and distributors, attempting to raise funds — Moore would never have been in Los Angeles to accept the call from NBC asking if he had any television ideas.

Moore had been asked before if he was interested in television. Warner Bros. television would have been the most likely candidate to persuade Moore and Glynn, but following on the heels of *Roger & Me*, he had no interest. It was only after *Canadian Bacon* had been written — and passed up by Warner Bros. and many other studios — that Moore became desperate enough to accept a meeting with NBC. More than a year had passed since he'd written the script for a movie that looked in serious danger of never being made. Penned during the summer of 1991, the Gulf War was still too fresh to mock. Moore rewrote the script approximately twenty times, and was still shopping it in November of '92.

It was during this period that a short sequel to *Roger & Me* was carried on PBS. During his days in Flint post-*Roger*, Moore had put together a twenty-three-minute update on his subjects, namely "Bunny Lady" Rhonna Britton, Sheriff Fred Ross, and Flint itself. After the PBS airing of *Pets and Meat: The Return to Flint*, Moore's office voicemail was full up. Naively he had included his actual telephone number in the film. "Three hundred and fourteen calls!" Moore reported. "And that's just the first day. Eighty per cent were people who lost their jobs and wanted to talk to me, but there were some — well, one guy needed help because he said there was a conspiracy against him involving the government and Sigourney Weaver." The segment was also released on VHS with shorts by three other comedy writers/filmmakers, including Steven Wright whom Moore would work with soon enough, on both *TV Nation* and *Canadian Bacon*.

An attempt at a *Dr. Strangelove* satire, Moore would

later describe the movie, hopefully, as "the first left-wing film for the mall crowd." Eventually the film would follow the screenplay and include sought-after comic actors John Candy, Alan Alda, Rhea Perlman, Rip Torn, and the aforementioned Wright, as well as cameos by James Belushi, Wallace Shawn, Dan Aykroyd, and of course, Moore himself. Alda, a U.S. president facing falling approval ratings, would decide to concoct a war with the country's neighbor to the north. In his very last role, Candy would star as Sheriff Bud B. Boomer of Niagara Falls, intent on leading a full-scale attack on Canada. The plot grew from Moore's concern "with the Gulf War and how quickly the people got behind this thing." "After the lessons of Vietnam I would think we should really be asking a lot of serious questions anytime someone says let's go to war," Moore stated. "Is that the only way we can exist, that we have to have a war-based economy, whether it's Cold War or not?"

In spite of Moore's passion for it, *Canadian Bacon* would be forced to take the back burner, and would not see release until 1995. To get the movie off the ground, he needed money. Realizing this, Moore lied his way into his meeting with Eric Tannenbaum, president of Columbia TriStar Television, and NBC's president Warren Littlefield by agreeing that yes, he had television ideas. On the way over to the studio in Burbank, California, Moore cranked the Metallica, and thought fast. He and Glynn devised the newsmagazine concept of *TV Nation*. With its straight-up politics and anticorporate stance, they were certain it would never be able to find advertisers, and would never catch on with the execs. They were wrong. In *Adventures in a TV Nation*, Moore described the idea thusly: "The show would be the most liberal thing ever seen on TV. In fact, it would go beyond 'liberals' because liberals are a bunch of wimps and haven't gotten us anything. This show would boldly go where no one has gone before." The reaction? "Smiles in the room. 'Tell us more!'"

Moore pitched in a fury, pulling out the riskiest ideas. But the executives kept smiling. They were excited by the idea of a show with real-looking correspondents, and even — or especially — the pitch for the pilot episode, "A Consumers Guide to the Confessional." This hellbent project was given a green light, and a budget of $1 million for the show's pilot. Given Moore's deep-rooted Catholicism, he sought out fellow fallen Catholic Janeane Garofalo to complete the survey of Hail Mary huts. Production commenced in January 1993.

In addition to Garofalo, Moore and Glynn rounded up satirical filmmaker Rusty Cundieff and *Late Night With David Letterman*'s Merrill Markoe to serve as reporters or correspondents. Each hour-long show was to have several segments, as well as the polls conducted by Robin Widgery, who had his own polling company in Flint. Moore was serious about employing people from his hometown where he could. He also hired Ben Hamper as a correspondent, saying, "It's my goal in life to keep him employed. . . . If you're a friend of mine, or a family member, I will try to keep you employed. I don't know if you can pay the rent on it, but I will try to work in all friends and relatives."

There were also regular casting sessions, and Moore and Glynn admitted that casting for a nonexistent show was difficult. As Derevlany (who would join the crew later) remembers, "Michael tried to staff the show with a mix of comedy writers and these earnest, humorless documentarians and political activists. I, fortunately, had sort of a mix of both backgrounds." Derevlany had worked for "a show on a fledgling comedy channel called Comedy Central. The show was called *Night After Night*, and it folded at the end of 1993. A bunch of people from that program went on to work on the first season of *TV Nation* as producers, researchers, associate producers, etc. The TV industry in New York City is surprisingly small. There are only a handful of shows going on, so everyone pretty much just goes from show to show."

With a quality crew in place, and the pilot completed within three months, there was just one problem for Moore: getting *TV Nation* on the air. The pilot was a success with NBC executives, a focus group, and a test audience in Scranton, Pennsylvania. However, a lack of space in the 1993 fall schedule left it sitting on the shelf. Moore returned to *Canadian Bacon* and, using the pilot as his new calling card, was able to secure Candy and Alda to star.

"I didn't understand a central fact about Hollywood ... which is that it doesn't matter how good the script is," Moore said. "What matters is who's in it, and will people pay money to go see them? I had my list of people I wanted to be in this film, but I never thought of actually going to the actors first."

With Candy and Alda secured, the Moore and Glynn fundraising team swung into action, using personalities to secure a future for their fictional war on Canada. Again relying on pop stars, Moore found material support in the Material Girl. He had long admired Madonna; during his days with the *Voice*, he ran an article about her image that defended the satirical intent of her then-new hit song,

"Material Girl." As luck would have it, Madonna, a Michigan girl at heart, had been affected by *Roger & Me*; its portrayal of Flint was something she could relate to, as her own hometown of Pontiac was less than forty-five miles away. Not only did Madonna contribute money to *Canadian Bacon*, her production company, Maverick Picture Company, got behind the picture in a way that it would with only handful of titles in the 1990s — including Madonna's own starring film of the same time, *Dangerous Game*. Madonna's manager Freddy De Mann also contributed to *Canadian Bacon*, and was named a producer.

Shooting on *Canadian Bacon* began in Toronto in mid-November 1993, with five-time Academy Award nominee (and two-time winner) director of photography Haskell Wexler at the helm. Walter Gasparovic was the film's assistant director. Though he later went on to partner on repeat projects with David Cronenberg, at that time Gasparovic had never met Moore. He came to the film by way of producer Stuart Besser and associate director Terry Miller — and on the basis of the script's humor. When I contacted Gasparovic he remembered, "production, like all productions, was full of challenges and hurdles — I do recall a lot of laughter on the set. Michael was new to fiction, but his sense of comedy helped him adapt to the day-to-day structure of shooting a nondocumentary."

"It's easier than nonfiction . . ." Moore said at the time about switching between forms. "You can make it up. You've got a blueprint called a script, and the actors will actually say what you tell them to say! With nonfiction, you don't have a clue what's going to happen." But in spite of Moore's good humor regarding *Canadian Bacon*, the brakes were slammed again. . . .

The BBC wanted *TV Nation*, and had agreed to share the cost with NBC. A man named Michael Jackson, head of U.K.'s BBC-2, had requested to see the pilot based on a gossip bit he read in *TV Guide*. As a result of his interest, the show would now play on not one, but *two* major television networks. It would hit as a summer show in the U.S. Moore got the congratulatory phone call on Boxing Day night, 1993. A new year began, and in January 1994, Moore and Glynn were off to New York to set up the official *TV Nation* offices.

On the first day of work, Moore and Glynn issued the following pep talk: "All of us need to behave as if we'll never work in television again. Because, if we do this show right, nobody will ever want us. It will be too dangerous to have us around. 'Oh, you worked on that show that pissed off the sponsors!' That's what they'll say." Those with future dreams of working on *20/20* and *Live with Regis and Kathie Lee* were told that *TV Nation* was not the place to build a résumé, and were asked to leave. "We will not make any friends in Congress or Corporate America. We will not lie to the viewer," Moore told his staff. "This is a rare chance for all of us who usually do not have a voice in the media to have our voices heard." Moore repeated this message throughout the show's run, for when Derevlany came onboard at the end of the first NBC season (as a six-week temp writer, and later, when the show switched to the Fox network, as Crackers himself), Moore was still holding to the motto.

Though Derevlany found Moore difficult to work with, he still values the sentiment today. "This is rare in TV, where everyone is ALWAYS angling for their next job and career move. It's great advice, and I still follow it. . . ."

Before breaking into television, Derevlany worked as both an investigative journalist and a comedy writer. He worked for New Jersey newspapers the *Hoboken Reporter* and the *Hudson Reporter*, and won a series of journalism awards. He founded his own short-lived comedy newspaper, the *Hoboken Review*, and became a contributing editor to the satirical magazine *National Lampoon*. He had also written for the *Village Voice*, and had a background in political organizing — all by the age of twenty-six. The *National Lampoon* job led Derevlany to the aforementioned *Night After Night* on Comedy Central. When the show folded at the end of 1993, and many of the writers joined *TV Nation*, Derevlany went west. In Los Angeles, he worked on a variety of short-lived shows, including *This Just In*, a news parody project on ABC.

Derevlany recalled, "Somehow, in the fall of 1994, I ran into one of the people I knew from Comedy Central who had been working on *TV Nation*. I heard from them that they were looking for writers. I got an address and sent in some material — some newspaper articles I'd written, videos, etc. I may have sent some ideas, too, I'm not sure. I guess my background seemed right, and then Michael gave me a call, and we chatted. I think I pitched some ideas. Most of them landed flat. But he was a fan of that show, *This Just In*, I had worked on, and he invited me to come to some sort of brainstorming session two days from then in New York for an upcoming 'end-of-year' special on NBC." With no guarantee of a job or pay Derevlany jumped on the next flight. "It should be noted that I had also just finished making a short film," he said, "and was about $20,000 in debt — I had no money to pay my rent, let alone a plane ticket, but it seemed like a reasonable risk."

Derevlany pitched ideas that wound up on the series — such as hiring a rent-a-cop from a security company to protect the president — and some that didn't, such as having dictator/film buff Kim Jung II of North Korea issue his Oscar picks to *TV Nation*. While the show was still at NBC, Derevlany worked on the end-of-year special segments, which included a limo ride with a Jacuzzi on top for America's most hated (landlords, gym teachers, telemarketers, and Satanists) in honor of "Auld Lang Syne"; "Didn't Die in 1994," a reverse-obituary segment calling attention to those who had survived the year; a "New Jobs" feature exploring Scranton, Pennsylvania, and the new jobs that had (or hadn't) been created there during the first term of the Clinton administration; and a *TV Nation* fan favorite, "Corp Aid," a lengthy segment in which Moore attempted (in the spirit of holiday giving) to donate money to corporations such as Exxon and Pfizer who had been hard-hit by lawsuits.

By the time Derevlany joined the *TV Nation* team, the show had found its scientific formula. But the question is: when you're sending a squad of black cheerleaders into an Aryan Nations meeting (in the spirit of "Love Night," a give-and-you-shall-receive style of confrontation), or asking a giant chicken to disrupt a newspaper strike in America's toughest city, how smoothly can one expect the television machine to operate? The show consisted of five eight-minute segments, along with introductions delivered by Moore, and the fill-ins featuring Widgery's outlandish stats. According to Derevlany, "all *TV Nation* stories were assigned to correspondents. Michael was supposed to be the correspondent for the Crackers pieces. Typically one writer was assigned to each of the segments — unless it was Michael's piece. Then ALL the writers had to go out." The sketches were roughly scripted ahead of time: "We had a basic beginning, middle, and end — although pieces frequently took on a life of their own and those original scripts were tossed out. In the field, the writers would feed the correspondent jokes, as well as make directing suggestions (writers on *TV Nation* were more like directors or codirectors with the field producers)." With all writers onhand for Crackers segments, lines would have to be fed to the giant chicken by shouting into the "ear" of the person wearing the suit — to tell him what to do or say. Obviously this situation was not ideal.

Moore and *TV Nation* had hired someone to design the Crackers bird suit — "a giant, unwieldy, badly built contraption," according to Derevlany. At this point, someone else was playing the part of the mascot. "After the first Crackers piece," Derevlany recalled, "we realized the person playing Crackers wasn't quite as smart or aggressive as we would like. I was personally very frustrated with having to spoon-feed that Crackers his every move. Instead of shouting in his ear, I suggested it would be easier for me to just put on the suit myself. Michael thought it was a good idea, because he thought I had a funny voice. I'm not sure if this is a good thing or not."

Derevlany was auditioned in the outfit, a test shot of Crackers attempting to bust into a movie theater — perhaps something to do with high ticket prices. Derevlany landed the gig and moved from a writer who had been hired on at the bare minimum amount the Writers Guild would allow, to Crackers, an important correspondent and character unlike any other on the program. His first assignment? The Philadelphia CoreStates bounced-checks bit. Derevlany remembers the experience was quite amusing: "I am not an actor. Or a puppeteer. I'm not even much of a performer. . . . Man, that suit was a fucking nightmare to wear. The head weighed a ton, and every time you moved, the chinstrap would slip over your neck and start to choke you. You couldn't really see anything. And your body was covered in sweat within moments of putting it on."

Looking back, Derevlany is aghast at what he and the crew were willing to do for the sake of comedy. "I later went on to work at a job with the Jim Henson Company, where I learned that suit performers — like Crackers — never spend more than a few minutes in their suit because their core body temperature rises to lethal levels within twenty minutes. And that's in an air-conditioned studio. I used to spend about ten hours a day in 100-degree Midwestern heat in that suit, with infrequent breaks." Even at the time, Derevlany was quick to search for solutions: "I had them install a small fan in the head, but we couldn't keep it on because we needed clean audio for me speaking. I would sometimes keep the suit on for more than an hour or two. If you see me doing anything funny on camera, it's mostly due to heat delirium."

Derevlany detailed another risk taken by the riskiest show on-air: "The biggest problem was having to drive that big Crackers mobile (a giant RV) while wearing the chicken suit (which was very hard to see out of). I still can't believe they made me do that, especially when I had to maneuver the vehicle through a crowd of about 500 people waiting to see the chicken."

"I did my thing on that first piece, and led a crowd of chanting people to a nearby bank, where I barged in and tried to open a checking account (in the chicken suit). At the time, Michael and his wife/producer Kathleen had this kind of shocked/horrified expression on their faces, and I thought I was doing something wrong. But I kept going because, well . . . I was having fun. Afterwards, I learned the expression was actually good 'shock,' as in, 'I can't believe how far he is taking this.'"

"From that point on, Crackers became more of a correspondent than a mascot, and my Summer of the Chicken began," Derevlany said. "Basically, Michael had been scheduled to do a bunch of pieces, but was often too busy (or too lazy?), so he would just send out the chicken instead. Which was fine with me. Although the hours were long and the suit was deadly, I loved the job, and they pretty much let me do whatever I wanted, which is a little crazy in retrospect. It's still one of my best jobs ever, even though it practically killed me."

Moore and Glynn acknowledged Crackers' cooling problem in their book, writing good-naturedly about taking Crackers to a Detroit Tigers' baseball game where Moore was to sing the Canadian national anthem as part of a "Canada Night" segment, to air August 25, 1995. According to them, it was during the game that Crackers met the Tigers' mascot and swapped stories, learning that other mascots had cooling systems — and demanding his own. Moore and Glynn continued in a G-rated version of the ball game, with Crackers signing autographs for kids. Derevlany said Detroit was tough on him from one side of town to the other: apparently the kids wanted to determine if the chicken had the actual "cojones" associated with the show.

"I did an appearance at a baseball stadium where a bunch of kids punched me in the nuts," Derevlany joked. And that wound up being the least of Crackers' problems in Detroit, where the whole crew weathered a beating.

Derevlany was accustomed to playing a bit rough. He had spent his teen years in the New York hardcore punk scene of the late '70s and early '80s. "So throwing myself physically into a piece was not that big a deal (I was WAY ahead of all those *Jackass* MTV-style shows). In fact, I was actually surprised people on the show weren't more aggressive (especially that first Crackers). I even thought Michael was a bit of a softy — he's much more gentle in real life than he comes across on TV," Derevlany said. "I, on the other hand, thought the people we went after were real scumbags and deserved to have a seven-foot chicken hurled at them."

As a matter of course, people did play a little rough with the chicken. During *TV Nation*'s Fox season, an ex-con named Louie Bruno was featured in several segments: once as a white man hailing a taxi cab (and getting chosen for pick-up over award-winning black actor Yaphet Kotto 99% of the time); on another episode as a candidate for president, campaign courtesy of *TV Nation*. At one point, Bruno hauled off and clocked Derevlany in the noggin. But that was nothing compared to what happened in Detroit. While nosing about the *Detroit News* and *Detroit Free Press* buildings while both news sources were on strike, the chicken was thrown approximately ten feet.

"It was one of the craziest things I'd ever seen," Derevlany confided. "This mob of striking newspaper workers and the hired management goons just started going at it at one point. There was no buildup of aggression, with some shouts and pushes. It was like — DING! DING! And everyone started swinging. Me and Michael, and the cameraman and sound person were at the front of the crowd. Michael, as usual, was buffeted by a couple of security people (who you never seem to see on camera). I was protected by my suit, more or less. The sound and cameraman, however, were actually getting their asses kicked. These management goons were wailing on their backs. So I had to do something. I ran into this garage, mostly to deflect attention from my crew, and the next thing I knew, I was being thrown backwards by the goons.

"The rest is a bit of a blur," Derevlany admitted, "but I remember wobbling back into the crowd, and this little child looking up at me saying, 'Please, Mister Chicken, don't cause trouble or people will get hurt.' It was completely surreal."

Apparently the Detroit newspaper management came from a burlier stock than did those of Philadelphia's banks. Later that day, Derevlany's elbow had "swollen up to the size of a grapefruit. It had somehow been injured in the melee. Unfortunately, I still had the piece to finish, which involved riding a bicycle in that damn suit, too. I eventually went to the hospital and got some ice packs and antibiotics."

When production for *TV Nation* wasn't physically dangerous, there were other hurdles to overcome. "I don't know if it's too political, but it's just a difficult show," said Moore regarding the show's bouncing from one network to another. "It's difficult to work with, makes people nervous." On the Crackers segments, Derevlany often had to re-dub lines in postproduction. "You can tell if you listen closely to the sound on the episodes. Mostly I had to change lines from 'corporate crime' to 'corporate wrong-doing,'" Derevlany said. "Apparently you can get sued for accusing someone of 'corporate crime,' but 'corporate wrongdoing' is vague enough to withstand a challenge."

TV Nation also had clever lawyers working for it, reminding the crew to do certain things to avoid arrest — like when the Greenwich beach party hit the shores of Connecticut, and crew members had to stay inside the high-tide line because, according to Moore and Glynn, "public trust doctrine says that the federal government actually owns the water, if not the sand, along any coast." Though Garofalo's beach party army was stopped by police and an aggressive Coast Guard boat before the crew could ever reach the shore, the media mutineers knew their rights, and were permitted to swim to shore and carry out their mission. There were also plenty of ideas and segments that never made it to viewers' homes. In their follow-up book, *Adventures in a TV Nation*, Moore and Glynn outline one of the segments that was cut — right off the bat — from the pilot and very first episode. The piece was called "Lie of the Week." The plan was to attach a voice-activated lie detector to a television, and find out what the news was really made of. "Either the machine didn't work that well, or the network news division had some explainin' to do, because when we tested this, the machine registered a lie in nearly every report on the news," they wrote. "Needless to say, the plug was pulled on this segment."

The show was production-heavy, and took up all of the months leading up to the air-date (July 19, 1994) to produce just eight episodes. Moore acknowledged that if it had been made a regular weekly show, it likely would have been too labor-intensive to work. *TV Nation* appeared nine times on NBC and developed a devoted following during the summer of '94. It won an Emmy that year for Best Informational Series, but was not renewed by the network. Its return the following summer was not on NBC, but on Fox. The *American Journalism Review* reported that the show was "scheduled to return this summer [1995] on Fox, which lured Moore away from NBC with promises of a weekly time slot and more creative freedom." "Lured" was perhaps a generous word for it, and though television continued to be a pleasant surprise for Moore, Fox did not turn out to be so free and loose after all. The network supported *TV Nation*, but, as Moore told the *Washington Free Press*, "We had constant, constant run-ins. Fox was very strict, and went over everything very closely." By contrast, NBC had objected to two pieces but, for the most part, left Moore to his own devices. A lighthearted Ben Hamper segment on why condoms are not available in size "small" was cut because NBC felt affiliates from the southern states might withdraw their supp;ort if the mental image of petite penises were conjured up for a full seven minutes. The piece did play on BBC, and again on Fox, but Fox had its own kinds of reservations and tended toward more serious censorship.

The Fox network didn't always understand the humor behind the show, or at least found it tasteless enough to cause worry regarding advertising and ratings. One contentious segment involved a Civil War reenactment group *TV Nation* hired to act out the bombing of Hiroshima, the fall of Saigon, and the riots in L.A. after the Rodney King verdict — all in full Civil War regalia. According to Moore and Glynn, Fox found the entire reenactment series "sick," so much so that they stipulated Moore himself introduce the segments as such. The L.A. riot segment — which included three parts: beating, verdict, and ensuing street chaos — was yanked entirely. A "Where are they now?" segment on the architects of the '80s savings and loan scandal was also cut, Moore suspected because the subjects who had allowed themselves to be filmed in a support group later changed their minds. Again due to an anticipated lack of support from advertisers, "Gay Bashing in Topeka" — a probing political piece about a boy who allegedly received extra credit from his high school for picketing the funerals of AIDS victims on behalf of God — would be barred from airing on Fox, though it would appear on the VHS version of the show and Moore would use the material again later on *The Awful Truth*. The only "gay issue" segment to run on Fox would be one pertaining to Senator Jesse Helms. One of the most controversial segments — and the most dangerous — was definitely this episode, known as "Love Night."

"Love Night" aired as the fourth *TV Nation* show on Fox, August 18, 1995. The idea was to ridicule hate groups by sending them love, following the Beatles' notion that "All You Need Is Love." *TV Nation* chose four hate movements they could approach: the Ku Klux Klan, who were holding a rally in Georgia; Aryan Nations, who were holding a convention in Idaho; anti-abortion group Operation Rescue, via their head officer's home; and North Carolina Senator Jesse Helms himself, who had consistently and stridently spoken out against gay men on the floor of the Senate and opposed bills designed to help people with AIDS.

For the Ku Klux Klan, a Mexican-American mariachi band and a troupe of black cheerleaders from a local college were delivered by *TV Nation* with love, along with roses, heart-shaped balloons, and a kissing booth. Along with hurling racial epithets, the white supremacists resorted to pushing and shoving, but the local police had assured the protection of the dancers and musicians, and in the end, the Klan departed, their racial taunts drowned out by a crowd of townspeople who had seen the cameras and commotion and had gathered to *laugh* at the hate group. The meeting with Aryan World Congress did not go so smoothly. *TV Nation*'s dream of delivering a mass quantity of love notes to the compound by air-drop faded after nineteen pilots turned the television show down. One agreed to the mission, but changed his mind when a sniper was spotted in a tower on the Aryan compound. Instead, a multiracial line of dancers was hired to shake their stuff and sing the Supremes' "Stop! In the Name of Love." Though *TV Nation* had arranged for security, there were no police on hand. The *TV Nation* security guards, against instructions and to Moore's chagrin, came armed with guns. Moore watched the tension escalate as the uniformed Nazis saluted the dancers Hitler-style, and skinheads smashed across the road to head-butt the cameras. The police arrived in the nick of time.

The Operation Rescue and Senator Jesse Helms visits were less tense, but no less controversial. The Helms home was presented with a strolling gay men's chorus singing "On the Street Where You Live," which Mrs. Helms politely acknowledged. For Operation Rescue, borrowing the tactics of the extremist faction of right-to-lifers — who staged pickets outside of abortion doctors' personal homes, leading to harassment, death threats, assaults, the occasional murder attempt, and vandalism — *TV Nation* bussed a

EMILY SCHULTZ

group of pro-choice feminists to plant flowers in the garden of a prominent antichoice lobbyist, who came out and — missing the irony — angrily tramped the flowers into the earth.

Of the four segments, it was the peaceful, flower-planting pro-choicers who were least likely to air. In all cases, Fox was concerned about giving publicity to hate groups, but also that the segments would result in harassment. They also feared losing advertisers. With the bit a personal favorite, Moore and Glynn went back and forth with the network's Standards and Practices department, attempting to convince them to let Love be. Finally, the network agreed to air all segments except the one on abortion — a topic they had already requested *TV Nation* avoid. Two of the five swastikas in the white supremacist segment were removed, and the word "gook" —which was perceptible three times — was covered once by an audio dog bark.

In the end, because of the show's length, the abortion segment of "Love Night" was not actually aborted. It ran in a shortened, softened form, a disclaimer added disavowing Operation Rescue from the mainstream Right-to-Life movement. This was not the first time Moore and *TV Nation* had run up against opposition on the abortion issue. While with NBC in '94, another segment on abortion had been cut. Not only did it never air, it was seized by the Secret Service for investigation. As Marvin Kitman of *Newsday* wrote: "Moore and his guerrilla band of para-journalists had spent a few days hanging out with one of the leaders of the anti-abortion movement, some of whose members believe abortion doctors should be killed. They made the rounds with him to the abortion clinics where he shouts down women. It was a very power-ful piece. But NBC felt it was going to lose advertisers because the piece was (1) about abortion and (2) anti-abor-tion. Actually, the piece was anti-killing doctors. What was the balance on the story? Moore argued, 'Is the other side of the issue arguing to let them kill doctors?'"

An Associated Press article by Lynn Elber, a television writer in Pasadena, California, shed more light on the seriousness of the scandal: "The Secret Service wants to review an unaired TV interview with an abortion foe who said the assassination of President Clinton and Supreme Court justices could be justified for the cause." That abor-tion foe was Roy McMillan, head of the Christian Action Group in Jackson, Mississippi, who claimed he had been misquoted in the transcript of the interview he did for *TV Nation*. McMillan's interview was taped while the show was still with NBC — who pulled the segment from the December 28 show, Moore said, because there wasn't enough time to find advertising for such a controversial subject during the holidays. Moore claimed the piece was not cut due to content. Yet it was a tumultuous time and tensions among antichoice groups were obviously run-ning high. Only two days after the segment was scratched from the schedule, two family planning clinics in Brook-line, Massachusetts, came under fire. Two people were killed and five were wounded. John C. Salvi III, a beauty-school student from New Hampshire, was charged. He was one of thirty who had signed a petition declaring deadly force justifiable in defense of the unborn. Paul Hill, who circulated the petition, was later convicted in Florida for two murders outside a Pensacola clinic.

"We'd like to review the transcript ourselves and see

the context in which the remarks were made. And that's what we'll try to do," the Secret Service's Harnischfeger was quoted as saying in Elber's article. "According to the transcript, McMillan was asked: 'Do you think it would be justifiable homicide to execute the president?' 'I think he's probably in harm's way by acknowledging and endorsing the killing . . . It would probably be to me more justifiable to assassinate the Supreme Court judges,' he said in the transcript." But McMillan told reporter Elber that "he was interviewed for hours and 'many hypothetical and leading questions' were asked."

Perhaps distracted by *TV Nation* and the hubbub and issues surrounding it, Moore's *Canadian Bacon* project received, if not less attention, a less than judicious eye. With 120 people, Moore shot the movie hopscotching between Toronto and Niagara Falls. Beginning with a country version of "God Bless America," inside the first five minutes the movie lapsed into American adages like turning "lemons into lemonade," and Candy and Perlman burst into a version of "High Hopes," the treacly song about a happy ant who thinks it can move a rubber tree plant a thousand times its size. A tribute to Moore's Canadian grandfather, the movie was intended as a spoof, of course, but perhaps not one that amused Americans living farther than 100 miles from the Canadian border. For example, when Candy starts a fistfight at a hockey game by saying that Canadian beer sucks, the president's people decide Canada might not be so bad an enemy — something the president badly needs for a boost in his approval ratings. They look for suspicious Canadian activity (the Niagara Falls blackout, the height of the CN Tower, the metric system, Neil Young, antislavery, and a socialist government). As Candy's character, Sheriff Bud B. Boomer, and his troops gaze upon the city of Toronto, they pronounce it the most beautiful city they've ever seen: "Like Albany, only cleaner." Upon breaking into a hydro plant in Niagara Falls, Canada, Boomer shouts: "There's not a locked door in the whole country!" An elderly couple, knitting and drinking tea, mind all of Canada's power. "We've got ways of making you pronounce the letter O," threatens Boomer. To this day, the film remains funny, but by no means the political *Strangelove* masterpiece Moore hoped it would be.

Kevin Mattson, a teacher of American History at Ohio University, author of *Intellectuals in Action*, and coeditor of an academic, labor-movement book called *Steal This University*, recently wrote in *Dissent Magazine*: "One of [Moore's] least-discussed projects, *Canadian Bacon*, captures the depth of his cynicism. Moore was writer, producer, and director of this fictional movie that's intended as political commentary." Mattson goes on to discuss the lack of solutions provided in Moore's work at large. Pointing to other popular television programs of the time, including *Beavis and Butthead*, *Married With Children*, and *Seinfeld*, Mattson cited cultural critic Mark Crispin Miller's notion of "'hipness unto death' and ironic detachment prominent among television watchers." Mattson pointed out, "as television deflates, the viewer wants to avoid being conned, thus rejecting anyone's claim to truth and embracing cynicism instead."

During *TV Nation*'s run, Moore was often criticized for making light of serious situations. The program was compared to *The Gong Show* and *Candid Camera* by television critic Tom Shales of the *Washington Post*, who, after viewing the very first episode, wrote that Moore's habit of "dragging people in front of a camera lens and humiliating them" was "neither a very noble calling nor a sufficient basis for a network TV show." Even today, discussions of *TV Nation* inspire both passion and contempt from the viewing public; on a popular Internet site called Jump The Shark, viewers battle back and forth on whether the program sold out with its very first episode, or not at all (so far, majority ruling is by 60 percent that the program never "jumped the shark" — i.e. sold out). Though the *TV Nation* concept was praised by Moore's old ball-and-chain, *Mother Jones*, the media critic at the *Village Voice*, James Ledbetter, wrote that the program's "chief shortcoming is that Moore has not evolved beyond the persona that he created for *Roger & Me*. After a while, harping on people with the mentality of a local consumer reporter ceases to have the same impact."

Moore, like much of the left in the 1970s, spent a great deal of time (as his *Voice* work can attest) offering workable solutions to social ills, only to find the grassroots movement fragmented by infighting in the 1980s. Moore's brief and explosive stint at *Mother Jones* is an excellent example of this broader about-face. "Solutions" notwithstanding, Moore, in his odd, accidental choice of television, had found his voice as a satirist whose edgy taste and use of catchy and quick editing found an audience with the growing alternative culture of the mid-'90s. At roughly the same time as Kurt Cobain's anthems of alienation started to reach thousands of listeners, *Roger & Me* became a cult hit, then a popular one. By the time *TV Nation* reached the airwaves only a few years later, political activism — from the Manic-Panic-ed feminism of the

Riot Grrrls to the growing antiglobalization movement — was reinvigorated on a mass scale. Indeed, with an amped Joan Jett on the White House mall, sing-shouting to a million NOW and NARAL supporters, left politics had become as simple as rock and roll again. Unlike many of his own contemporaries, Moore could speak to this new movement.

According to Mattson's argument in *Dissent Magazine*, "Moore has done something the left rarely does. He's made political criticism entertaining. And as polls show, Generation X and Y Americans get their news increasingly from entertainment shows — the hip irony of political jokes told on *The Late Show With David Letterman* and *The Daily Show With Jon Stewart*. Indeed, when Moore's *TV Nation* broadcast on NBC and Fox in 1994–1995, the demographic reports showed that a large number of the eighteen to thirty-four-year-old crowd was tuning in. Moore's success illustrates how young people are reached via satellite dishes and mega-mall bookstores rather than through cafés or union halls or small magazines."

Mattson raises excellent points about cynicism in the left, ending with the question: "What happens to the vision of the left when it plays on the grounds of the sound-bite society," but Moore himself has not shied away from discussions of cynicism. The ending of *Canadian Bacon* shows Hacker Corp, in charge of all of America's missiles, programming them to launch — aimed for the CN Tower where Bud B. Boomer's officer Honey (Perlman) is stationed. Alda must attempt to negotiate a ceasefire with Hacker Corp in dollars and cents. The point? Corporations have more power than the president or national defense. Upon the release of

Canadian Bacon, Moore acknowledged the film's pessimism. "Underlying the humor, though, is a very serious point, and underneath that is a lot of anger," he said. "I think some of the best comedy comes from people who are very angry about the situations they see in the world, and the humor sort of acts as a means to deal with the frustration of living in the society in which we live."

On March 4, 1994, something more personally frustrating occurred: John Candy died of a heart attack. With him, Moore's film also died. "What I most remember about the shoot is the absolute pleasure it was to work with John Candy," Walter Gasparovic, *Canadian Bacon*'s associate director, told me during our E-mail interview. "In my career, I have not met an actor as loving and warm." Not only was the cast devastated, the film was incomplete. Major problems were left to be solved in editing, and, with the company's lack of support through final production, the result was a movie that scanned as a rough cut rather than a finished film. According to an interview with Moore from the time, further complicating the film were "studio bosses who wanted to exploit Candy's last performance by 'dumping in as much of him as possible' at the expense of more serious subtexts."

"From the beginning, there was a difference in the type of film Michael wanted to shoot and the type of film the studio wanted," explained Gasparovic. "I believe Michael wanted more of a satire in the vein of *Dr. Strangelove* (one of his favorite films) and the studio felt they needed more schtick with Candy and cast. I believe this discrepancy was also evident in the promotion, or lack thereof."

In reality, *Canadian Bacon* was barely released. It opened September 22, 1995 — in fourteen theaters. It never made it to the malls, as Moore had hoped. Moore claimed the studio buried it promotion-wise, and he was right. In the end, according to the Web site Box Office Mojo, the film grossed only $163,971 in theaters. It did play major festivals, however, including those in Toronto and Cannes, and it sold an unexpected 200,000 copies on VHS. Moore is certainly not remembered by his fans for *Canadian Bacon*, but the film goes hand-in-hand with *TV Nation*. Together they led to the Moore the public now knows — not always well-liked, but always successful.

It is this Moore that *TV Nation*'s Derevlany commented on with some reluctance. "Let me just say that I still find Michael to be one of the most brilliant, funny, and most inspiring people I have ever met. Would I ever work for him again? No. I can't even watch his films. (I still haven't seen *Bowling for Columbine*, which I hear is quite good.) Knowing how miserable the process can be to make his projects, I'm still a little sensitive to what people probably had to suffer through to get the footage and make Michael — and Michael alone — look good."

After the *TV Nation* years, and an Emmy nomination for his work as Crackers, Derevlany was offered an abundance of work in children's television. He was employed by the Jim Henson Company for several years, and today still derives most of his income from children's programs, where he said he feels he makes more of an impact than he ever did on *TV Nation*. In spite of the suffering endured by the corporate crime-fighter, he did add a final salute to the show: "After *TV Nation*, I did get a lot of offers to do reality and prank shows, but they were all very disappointing. It was like, 'We play this trick on this guy — and then it's funny!' And my question would always be, 'Why? And then what?' There never was a 'then what.' At least on *TV Nation*, there was always a political point — or a point of some sort — to justify occasionally juvenile pranks and stunts. That's rare these days. Even on a brilliant show like *The Daily Show*, the segments are about getting laughs, not about making a point. *TV Nation* did both, and did it well."

As well as his voice, Moore had found his working method. He would use the same approach, and often the same staff, for the rest of the decade — into his successes of *The Awful Truth* and *Bowling for Columbine*. By the time *TV Nation* completed its run and went off the air, Moore was forty-one. Though he had begun his activist career at a tender age, by no means was he over the hill. He did, however, have a plan to cut the corporate "downsizing" trend down to size — with a pen, and again, his camera.

CHAPTER SIX

Biggie Up the Downsize

Book Signings, Road Food, and Nike

Call to mind forty-seven cities across the United States — or, in Michael Moore terms, the country that ought to give itself a makeover, starting by changing its name to "The Big One." Now imagine visiting this vast collection of metropolises within fifty days. Why? Because this was no ordinary book tour. This was a Michael Moore book tour.

After the summer of 1995, Moore's show *TV Nation* was let go by the Fox network. Though he had screenings of *Canadian Bacon* to premiere that fall, and speaking dates to bolster the movie's unfortunate lack of label-promotion, it became quickly apparent that Moore's second feature film was not going to be the runaway success that was *Roger & Me*. In disappointment, Moore turned back to his roots: writing. Michael's parents Frank and

Veronica had taught him to write before he had even entered grammar school, and by this point in his life, Moore had honed a political rant-style typhoon that was perfectly timed to the mid-'90s. The resulting tome, *Downsize This!*, summed up much of the work Moore had already done with *Roger & Me* and *TV Nation*. But it also, unexpectedly, lay the foundation for another film project — *The Big One*, a documentary about Moore himself on his book tour across the vast U.S. of A.

In the first few minutes of the film, a glum-looking Moore straggled down a city street, noting in voice-over, "Me, well, I've been out of work. So I did what most people like me do when they can't get a job. I wrote a book . . . *Downsize This! Random Threats From an Unarmed American*. I sold it to Random House. They asked me if I wouldn't mind going on a little author tour . . . say, four or five cities." Is this what most people do when they find themselves out of work? It's not, nor was Moore really out of work when he decided to pen his book. As a filmmaker, former publisher, political activist, and all-around media prankster, it's often hard to define oneself as "in work" or "out of work," but true to the factory terminology of the regular working-class Joe, Moore set up the parameters of both *Downsize This!* and *The Big One* in this manner — and to much success.

Releasing in the U.S. in September 1996, the book received a starred review in *Publishers Weekly* which described the book as "a mordant satire that will leave both conservatives and liberals reeling with embarrassment. . . . No one is immune; a scathing, funny book packed with facts, it will appeal to those who loved Al Franken's *Rush Limbaugh Is a Big Fat Idiot*." *Downsize*

EMILY SCHULTZ

This! held position on the *Publishers Weekly* nonfiction bestseller list for a notable four weeks.

But how did that "little author tour" Random House had arranged grow from several major American cities to most of America at large? Plain and simple: it was up-sized, Moore-style. Chronicled in the book was a prank called "Would Pat Buchanan Take a Check From Satan?" "Politicians, as we all know, will take a campaign contribution from wherever they can get it," wrote Moore in chapter two. "But will they really take a check from just anyone?" Setting up legitimate bank accounts using his assistant Gillian Aldrich's home address, Moore founded the John Wayne Gacey Fan Club, Satan Worshippers for Dole, and Abortionists for Buchanan, among others. Writing checks to Pat Buchanan on March 3, 1996, and May 8, 1996, the payments were put into the system and cashed within three and ten days respectively. Bob Dole and Ross Perot campaigns returned the suspicious checks that had landed in their offices, but like Buchanan aides, Bill Clinton's staff took the bait — from the Hemp Growers of America. With the release of *Downsize This!* during the two months leading up to the 1996 American presidential election, this particular trick brought the book to almost immediate national attention. Mike McCurry, a White House spokesperson, called Moore "a dangerous person," so Moore decided to enter his own platform which coincided with the electoral one — except that he wasn't running for anything, he was simply running against the "Republicrats," as he called them in the light-toned tome he was out to market. Moore added the smaller American cities he preferred, ones like Flint that had been most affected by downsizing, and others like Des Moines, the very hub of the American election. Moore had discovered a media tactic he could call upon again, every four years in fact (or every two, if he wanted to exploit the congressional elections). By pairing his art to an election, Moore ensured his work wasn't just *in* the news, it *was* news.

"I've always been a writer, and I haven't had the chance to do that in a while," Moore told the *Washington Free Press* while on tour. "As the year started to progress, it looked like we weren't going to get *TV Nation* on [the air] this year, and I thought, 'This is wrong. Here we are in an election year, and we're not on TV . . . So I went to what I guess was the only outlet available to me, which was just to start writing and try to get a book published." Before *Downsize This!* had even been completed, it earned Moore a six-figure contract for a follow-up, the Kathleen Glynn–cowritten *Adventures in a TV Nation*. In *Downsize This!*, the writing was pithy and comical, skipping from topic to topic much like Moore's stand-up routines, each chapter approximately four to ten pages long. Though not without its grim moments, *Downsize This!* was certainly less serious, less adamant, and less focused about its agenda than Moore's later books, *Stupid White Men*; *Dude, Where's My Country?*; *The Official Fahrenheit 9/11 Reader*; and *Will They Ever Trust Us Again?* Tongue planted firmly in cheek, Moore was out to dissect the effects of NAFTA, and put faces to the *TV Nation*–established concept of "corporate crooks," particularly in regard to their acceptance of state "welfare." At the same time, Moore hopscotched between a variety of pop-cultural and political issues, everything from chastising big business for its use of concentration camp labor during the Second World War, to attempting to prove that 1996 primaries' candidate Steve Forbes was an alien, and even examining Moore's own forbidden love of Hillary Rodham Clinton.

The film of Moore's book tour didn't actually begin until about halfway through the tour when, unbeknownst to his publisher, Moore called a four-person crew to join him in St. Louis. What happened while Moore was on the road to prompt him to call up BBC Productions and ask them to send out documentarians and pronto? Simple: Moore didn't like what he was seeing in the cities he visited.

"I was reading about the strong economy and record days on Wall Street, but seeing something much different in all these cities," Moore reported when he debuted *The Big One* nine months later in Flint. Of course Moore must have known what he would see. He had already seen it years earlier in Michigan, and prophesized its coming when he toured *Roger & Me* across the country in 1990. In fact, the title of his book, and the frontispiece photographs — comparing the collapsing government building in Oklahoma City after the 1995 bombing to a factory in Flint being destroyed after GM layoffs — show the false naivety Moore employed when presenting *The Big One* to audiences. If he hadn't known what he was going to encounter on his tour, would he have arranged to visit the smaller cities of Baltimore, Maryland; Centralia, Illinois; or Rockford, Illinois, which had just overtaken Flint in *Money* magazine for the worst place in America to live?

Even at this early point in his career, Moore was being pegged as a put-on Everyman, the *New York Times* predicting "Mr. Moore may not be able to maintain his image (pro-union, plain folks, blue collar, never went to college) much longer." While that was fine for the *New York Times* to print from its review desk, the majority of

Moore's book sales would come from working people, often in danger of losing their jobs. Though most didn't read the *New York Times* books pages, these readers' $21 apiece did contribute to putting *Downsize This!* on the *Times'* bestseller list.

On October 27, 1996, Moore stood in a parking lot in Milwaukee, Wisconsin, a cell phone in one hand, a tall cup of Wendy's soda in the other. "Oh my God! We've made the *New York Times* bestseller list!" he laughed heartily. "Oh man . . . oh my God, that's such good news." For a man whose television show had gone without renewal, whose last feature-length film had been buried by the studio, who was currently scheduled to be away from his wife and teenage daughter for eight consecutive weeks, and whose current feature depended upon success of the book, it was *indeed* good news! Moore's first thought was to ask if anyone had phoned his wife yet to let her know. In a few days, Glynn was scheduled to meet him in Chicago, where they would celebrate their anniversary together, borrowing a few precious hours away from Moore's intensive book tour. But for now, Moore stood in a Midwest parking lot with his crew, continuing with mild blasphemies, admitting, "I'm stunned."

Up until this point, the *Downsize* tour, like Moore's *Roger & Me* tour, seemed to include "the same twenty interviews with the same twenty questions." In big box bookstores, surrounded by cardboard cutouts of Tina Turner and Stephen King, Moore would continue signing for the store even after the crowd was gone, in the hopes that leaving behind signed copies would entice sales from those unable to attend the performance. As is common on road trips, Moore was beginning to get sick of the sight of himself: he pointed out the digital manicure Random House had given him on his cover photo, and wondered why the book designers couldn't have stripped an extra couple pounds off his face since they were already tinkering. Turning to the equally unshaven for comfort, Moore escaped into the strong voices of female pop-folk musicians Fiona Apple, Paula Cole, and *I Ain't A Pretty Girl*, Ani DiFranco. "I have never understood the shaving of the armpit," Moore would admit.

Lobbying in factory parking lots, talking to truckers and working moms at the Hearty Platter and other road-side stops about their voting intentions (or lack thereof) for the upcoming election (which would indeed wind up with the lowest voter turnout in American history), Moore had been becoming increasingly road-weary. *The Big One* showed Moore in interviews, performing the content of his book verbatim, both in front of live audiences and on radio shows. Showing up in a new city every day, following his "media escort" through endless halls, being admonished by them, and told that he needed a mother, finding a few lines of local content to include for each speaking engagement, and sneaking off when possible to present honors like the "Downsizer of the Year Award" to companies like Johnson Controls, PayDay candy bars, or Pillsbury, could not have been a barrel of laughs, no matter how lighthearted Moore appeared on film. When asked about the P.R. people he pestered during the tour, and whether he felt sorry for them, Moore was conflicted. "Look — they're workers too. The CEO won't come down and talk to me, so they've got to deal with me. So, I do feel bad for them on one level. . . . Every day, they sit in those cozy little offices and get softball questions from the mainstream press." Moore declared, "for one lousy day out of their lives, some overweight guy in a ball cap comes into the lobby and asks a simple question: How do you defend the position that the company just made a record profit and laid off ten thousand people? They know it's indefensible; they're not stupid."

In Chicago, Moore was interviewed by radio host and union man Studs Terkel, who pointed out that the images in the front of *Downsize This!* related to the question, "What is terrorism?" Moore replied, "Well, obviously, if you park a Ryder truck in front of a building, filled with explosives, and blow up that building and kill 168 people that's an act of terrorism. There's no question about that. But what do you call it, Studs, when you politely remove the people from the building first. . . ." Moore's point was that once a community's livelihood had been stripped, a number of people die, simply by other means — suicide, spousal abuse, drugs and alcoholism — the social problems that follow people who have become unemployed.

"We don't call the company a murderer. But I do consider this an act of economic terrorism when, at a time you're making a record profit, you would throw people out of work just so you can make a little bit more."

Having traveled across "The Big One" several times now, Moore was asking what, to his mind, was a simple question — Why would you lay off people if it was at all avoidable? But he had his own work cut out for him. From the moment Moore brought in the film crew, he was doing triple-duty in each city as author, filmmaker, and subject/star. *Salon* would later critique this kind of tri-sectional mirror as infinite ego and ultimate vanity — and another journalistic brouhaha would ensue. But between giving hugs to recently laid-off workers; getting his kicks by jamming with rock musician Rick Nielson of Cheap Trick in Rockford (Moore can actually remember more Bob Dylan lyrics than anyone has a right to); making a point by taking a fresh discharge from Johnson Controls to Manpower to try to get him temp work after twenty years as a full-time employee; and avoiding arrest outside LEAF industries by playing back video footage to police to prove that he and the crew had been instructed to wait outside rather than to leave; Moore also had to figure out how all of this would add up to a real movie, and hopefully, a commercially successful one. Said media escort Mary Gielow, "his is the most fly-by-the-seat-of-your-pants book tour I've ever seen — and I've been doing this for seven years. Things are just sort of scratched, and things are added, and people want him constantly . . . to chat with him, and he obliges, which is very nice but it throws the schedule a curve." When asked how that affected her life, she fired back, asking if she had developed a twitch yet.

While the media escorts were commandeering Moore, Moore was commanding his crew. "What's the deal here? We're not gonna get . . ." his cameraman protested at one point. Moore's firm response was always, "You never turn that camera off." Both camera operators obliged, one filming Moore, and the other filming the first cameraman.

Aside from the personal clashes that occur on any tour, there were also the disputes that were bound to emerge from an anticonglomerate author signed with a major publishing house and appearing at major chain book-stores. The trouble began in Philadelphia, where Borders bookstore workers were striking. A labor boy in spite of his *Downsize This!* chapter, "Why Are Union Leaders So F#!@ing Stupid?" Moore refused to cross the picket line. "I don't cross the picket line, so I asked if the protesters could come in for the reading," he said. "Borders approved this, as long as everyone behaved properly." Inviting the striking workers in allowed for the presence of one contested worker, Miriam Fried, whom it was rumored had been dismissed for her support of the union. Fried was allowed to speak. After this first incident, the *Philadelphia Inquirer* quoted a union official who said that Moore had urged the audience to buy their books at a competitor's store. Moore later denied this, saying he didn't want shoppers to boycott Borders, but Jody Kohn, a spokeswoman for the company, based in Ann Arbor, Michigan, backed up the original quote, "He said, 'Hey, there's a Rizzoli's down the street; you can shop there.'" Borders and Moore entered into a running conflict during which each accused the other of dishonesty.

Following on the heels of the Philadelphia appearance, Moore's World Trade Center Borders stop was also thrown askew. Moore claimed Borders officials had canceled his speech just hours ahead because they did not want a repeat of the previous event: "They told me I could sign the books, but I was not to open my mouth." Kohn chalked the cancellation up to Port Authority police asking the store to eliminate the "enormous" crowds from afternoon author sessions.

In Des Moines, as portrayed in *The Big One*, Moore was contacted by a group of Borders employees attempting to unionize. They nervously monitored cars driving through the parking lot as they met in secret one night with Moore. They joked that they were afraid of the possibility of a union-buster from Omaha, and confided that funds were being withdrawn from their checks for an HMO that did not have a doctor in Des Moines. This group of Borders workers would later vote the union in, on December 10, through the Food and Commercial Workers.

The last straw for Moore came in mid-November, when a Fort Lauderdale book signing was killed completely. According to Moore, "They said they'd received a directive from corporate headquarters that Michael Moore would not be allowed to speak at any Borders nationwide." In the *New York Times*, Kohn attributed the cancellation to a lack of scheduling confirmation. The *Sun-Sentinel* ran Moore's version impartially, while allowing it was possible that a local manager was unable to keep the numerous bookings straight. Either way, Moore was pissed off. In a column that appeared in *The Nation* on November 18, Moore contended that Borders had banned him en masse from appearing in their stores, and announced that he would donate the royalties from 1000 copies of his book to the union drive. With 8000 workers to be organized, and royalties ranging between 10 and 20% of list price, depending on the publishing contract (a value of between $2000 and $4500), the pledge amounted to 50 cents per worker. Given the number of copies Moore was selling at this time, this was a modest donation, but it was a symbolic gesture against a bookstore where he was scheduled to appear.

"I just don't think they're thinking very clearly now because they're so afraid," Moore said of Borders officials to the *New York Times*. "I was really looking forward to going out on a book tour. I'm not going out on a union-organizing tour." Borders' response was that Moore had a severe persecution complex. With a union drive affecting just four of their stores, and plenty of promotional dollars poured into *Downsize This!*, Borders officials stated that it would go against all sense for them to stifle the bestselling author of the season, and therefore one of their biggest sources of income. The sides reached a truce, and the downsized author continued his book tour, resuming his Borders appearances. The conflict, however, was far from over. Even as *The Big One* film was introduced at festivals the following summer, Moore was still fuming. As chronicled in Chapter Three ("Are You Going to San Francisco?"), in July 1997, Moore would call on the editor of *Salon*, writing: "As I read your libelous attack on me in *Salon* magazine, 'Moore Is Less,' I wondered, before you published it, did you ask yourself, 'Don't we have a moral responsibility to our readers to tell them who we are and why we are publishing this article?'"

Moore pointed out that *Salon* was "sponsored and presented by Borders Books and Music." Detailing his Borders conflict from the previous year, Moore extended his problem to include *Salon* by association: "*Salon* chose not to inform you of this. I believe that it was dishonest not to tell you that Borders, their sponsor, and I have been locked in this conflict. That they would use this magazine to libel me is a low blow from an otherwise respected bookseller."

Just what did this attack involve? An author named Daniel Radosh had penned a crucifixion of Moore's entire curriculum vitae to date. It headlined, "Five Reasons the Left Can Do Without Michael Moore," and answered in the first line, "1. Roger and Me, Me, Me, Me, Me!" The column pointed to the kinds of deception and self-promotion Moore had exhibited throughout his career, beginning with the lack of defined timeframe in *Roger & Me*, and moving to his short film, *Pets or Meat*, which Radosh saw as a patting-itself-on-the-back follow-up to *Roger & Me*. After dismissing *Canadian Bacon* without having viewed it, Radosh went on to discuss Moore's *TV Nation* work, as well as his "Media Matters" columns in *The Nation* — including the throwing down of the gauntlet on the Borders debacle — concluding that the only media that seemed to matter to Moore was his own.

The anger in Moore's response is palpable — he must have been reeling. Many of the charges leveled at Moore by Radosh have been repeated in the ensuing years, by respected lefty critics like Christopher Hitchens, and by concerned citizens of the right, armed with the power of the Internet, including such sites as Moorewatch.com and Moorelies.com, as well as the often inaccurate *Michael Moore Is a Big Fat Stupid White Man*, a book that confused the Flint suburb of Davison for that of its wealthy neighbor, Clarkston, Michigan, and built an entire theory upon the supposition. With that exception, many of the charges leveled at Moore are arguably true: Moore probably is too self-congratulatory; Moore probably overdoes the self-promotion in comparison to the norm for a lefty activist, the do-gooder who is supposed to be without personality or pride; Moore arguably *does* condescend in attempting to always keep his message simple; Moore has indeed become wealthy while still hanging on to his image as the regular Joe. Still, Radosh's column was contemptuous, rude, and taken as a whole, immature.

David Talbot, editor of *Salon*, showed no sympathy for Moore's pride at this first sting. He replied within the on-line magazine: "Moore's charge that the Borders bookstore chain 'use(d) this magazine to libel me' is outrageous and utterly false and I challenge him to offer proof of this. Yes, Borders is one of *Salon's* sponsors — this is emblazoned on our site, so we're not exactly hiding it from our readers. But none of *Salon's* editorial content is dictated by Borders or any of our other advertisers, nor has Borders ever attempted to influence *Salon's* reporting, criticism and commentary," Talbot continued. "Moore is swinging wildly here and he knows it."

The Moore vs. Borders dispute was left to languish while Moore prepared for the production and promotion of *The Big One*. He showed the film at Cannes in May, and in mid-July, took it to Flint to give his hometown a special viewing. In mid-September, the work was featured in the Independent Feature Film Market at the City Cinemas Angelika Film Center in New York, a kind of industry trade show and week of workshops. Though the lineup that year included more than 400 projects, Moore's was one of only sixty-six documentaries, and in fact, just one of ten feature-length docs. For the third time in eight years, as he entered the show, Moore was able to pin on the trademark "green badge" of the feature-length moviemaker. Though the IFFM was not the place to secure distribution, Moore knew he would find his company through BBC Productions, and he did. He secured distribution with the still-hot Miramax Films, producers of 1994's *Pulp Fiction* and 1997's *Chasing Amy*, which showed at IFFM that same year. On January 21, 1998, Moore found himself once again in documentary heaven, a.k.a. Park City, Utah's Sundance Film Festival. This time he and Glynn were chatting with David Mamet, who was there with *The Spanish Prisoner*. Other memorable films show-ing that year included Vincent Gallo's *Buffalo 66*; a second film starring Christina Ricci, *The Opposite of Sex*; *Kurt and Courtney*, by Nick Broomfield — yet another docu-mentary filmmaker known for including himself in his own films; as well as the drama with documentary roots, *Central Station*, by Walter Salles. Also featured was *Affliction*, a new film by Paul Schrader — the screenwriter of one of Moore's favorite movies, *Taxi Driver*.

Making its theater release a year after its completion, on April 10, 1998, the *New York Times* reviewed *The Big One* as "the rare mainstream American film about real issues, and the too-rare documentary with a reasonably commercial future." Things were looking up again for Moore. Although reviewer Janet Maslin was wrong in her predic-tion — domestic theater gross would wind up estimated at just under $1 million falling far short of *Roger & Me* — *The Big One* was well-received and Moore's confidence was up. He began writing a fiction picture for Channel Four Films in Britain; he signed up the still-unnamed con-tinuation of *TV Nation* (later dubbed *The Awful Truth*); he and Glynn finished up their next book, chronicling their first adventures in television; and he readied a sitcom pilot for CBS starring Jim Belushi, an *All in the Family*–style comedy called *Better Days*, set in a town without any jobs. Though half of these projects would go nowhere, Moore had an energy-in-motion vibe about him. As *The Big One* opened with wide release in April, Moore found himself in the midst of an absolute blitz of media and promotion.

Media blitz surrounding a road movie about a book? What was all the fuss about? The answer, strangely, was running shoes. Moore has said he had no idea that he would actually get an interview with Phil Knight, founder and CEO of Nike, Incorporated, and "Corporate Crook No. 3" in Moore's top ten list in *Downsize This!* Why Knight's Public Relations Director decided to phone up Portland's KXL 750AM, the radio station where Moore was a guest speaker, and invite him to drop by Nike headquarters on October 30, 1996, remains a mystery. With Portland as the last city featured in the film of Moore's book tour, there is no doubt that without the interview, which cinches the movie journey closed, there would have been little handle — or scandal — for the press to pick up on when attempting to give *The Big One* good face.

Moore told *Variety*, "[Knight] rarely gives interviews, and I don't know if he knew what he was getting into. . . . At one point, I asked how he felt making shoes in Indonesia using twelve-year-olds, and he said, 'They're not twelve, they're fourteen.' He was deadly serious." The scene in *The Big One* showed a Knight who was very comfortable talking to Moore and the camera — though he had no intention of accepting Moore's offer of plane tickets to Indonesia (a place he'd never been) to view his shoe factory suppliers.

"What drives me is not money. I'm not in this for money anymore," Knight said. "Basically what I want to do before I go to that Great Shoe Factory in the Sky is make this as good a company as I can make it. I simply have a basic belief having been burned on it once, and really believing it very strongly, that Americans *do not want* to make shoes." Though Knight did agree to consider it, he also was quite direct that he would be unlikely to set up a factory in Flint, as Moore proposed. Moore challenged him to a footrace, an arm wrestle for it, and in the end, settled for Knight's $10,000 matching of his own contribution to the Flint school system.

The New York Times called the movie loose-limbed, but also commended its energy: "A lively sparring match with Phil Knight, chairman of Nike Corporation, doesn't culminate in a Nike shoe plant for Flint, which is what Mr. Moore asks for. But it does find these two adversaries speaking face to face, if not eye to eye, about the kinds of labor issues that don't often make it to the multiplex. So at least it's a start."

Moore claimed Nike was upset about the film after seeing a bootleg copy. "They . . . called and said, 'We'd like to meet with you.' I thought they were going to tell me they're going to build the factory in Flint, where I challenged them to build one," Moore told Ian Hodder of *Industry Central: The Motion Picture and Television Industry's First Stop!* "Instead, their director of public relations flies to New York and takes me out to breakfast. I sit down at the table and he says to me, 'What would it take to have two scenes removed from the movie?'" Moore recalled that he "kind of freaked out. I didn't even want to hear what the offer was. I just said, 'Well, I'm not taking anything out of the movie. I'll add a scene. I'll add a scene of you building that factory in Flint.'"

According to Moore, the director of public relations said that Knight was upset with two things in the movie, feeling he had spoken unclearly and misrepresented himself. One issue was the age of the Indonesian workers. Knight had said it was fourteen but, in his second interview with Moore, corrected himself, changing it to sixteen. In the film, it remains fourteen. "The second thing," Moore paraphrased, "was, 'in five years, one of those poor little Indonesians is going to be your landlord.' They sort of figured out there's some subtle racism in that statement, and they wanted it out."

Both scenes remain in Moore's film.

In an article in *Dissent* magazine, Kevin Mattson argued, "Moore ends this final segment of [*The Big One*] by saying, 'I know what most of you're thinking: I sure would have liked to have seen that footrace. Well, maybe next movie.' Which, if I read him correctly, suggests that this confrontation has become a humorous bust — the problems of globalization remain while the audience awaits Moore's next bit of entertainment." Mattson may be correct in his assessment — that the majority of moviegoers, even the most intelligent, are simply looking for entertainment. Looking back at the spring of 1998, however, it did seem as if change was on the horizon.

Moore hit Portland running — just before his movie opened in New York and in theaters across the nation. He answered questions at a makeshift press conference at the Utopia coffee shop on Southeast Belmont Street, which was not so fancy-pants it couldn't include a local zine alongside newspapers. With its own premiere at the Bagdad Theater, sponsored by Portland Jobs With Justice, The Western States Center, and FM radio station KBOO, Moore arrived via limousine. He began the evening with an animated stand-up routine, calling anti-Nike senti-ment "the student movement of the late '90s." Of the brewpub/theater and sellout crowd, Moore said, "this is great . . . showing the movie to 600 drunk people. My movies go down better with beer," though Moore himself has been seldom known to drink. The film was greeted with whistles and hollers, particularly the end portion featuring Portland's own Knight of Nike. According to *Willamette Week*, a Portland alternative news weekly, "The audience wanted to know if Moore had met with any of the 250 Nike employees who were laid off less than a week earlier (he hadn't). They also wanted to know if Moore thought Knight was good or evil. ('He has a blind spot.')"

On May 13, Nike stated that it would increase the minimum age of hired workers, as well as raising air-quality standards in its Indonesia facilities to match those in the United States. According to the *New York Times*, "the company has been hurt by falling stock prices and weak sales even as it has been pummeled in the public relations arena, including ridicule in the comic strip *Doonesbury* and an encounter between Mr. Knight and the gadfly filmmaker Michael Moore in his new documentary, *The Big One*." Moore's film had opened in theaters barely one month earlier, but Knight attributed Nike's falling sales to financial crisis in Asia and a lack of understanding of the consumer trend toward hiking shoes. "'I truthfully don't think that there has been a material impact on Nike sales by the human rights attacks,' he said, citing the company's marketing studies." The *Times*, however, also pointed out that the company had begun to address complaints about employment practices after student groups demanded their universities hold advertiser Nike to higher standards.

The Big One would be forgotten, but six years later, *Downsize This!* would continue to turn profits, topping the *Der Spiegel* bestseller list in Germany. The book was reissued by Piper, a hundred-year-old boutique literary publisher known for being the first publisher to bring Dostoevsky to German readers many years ago. As America shuffled its downsized years under and trudged on, other countries would continue to find something in Moore's critical American sentiments, particularly after September 11, 2001, when the world beyond the United States would welcome all opposition to the Bush administration. In 2003, more than one million copies of *Downsize This!* had been sold in Germany, and in combination, Moore's *Downsize This!* and *Stupid White Men* remained on bestseller lists for ten consecutive months. *Publishers Weekly* reported on the Moore phenomenon there: "Germans, suffering from double-digit unemployment, cracks in its governing coalition, and a tortured debate over welfare reform, remain curiously obsessed with where someone else's country has gone. . . . True, Moore has done well for Penguin in the U.K., and for Crown, Harper, and now probably Warner in the U.S., as well as assorted publishers in Japan, France, Australia, and elsewhere. But the German sales figures are downright astonishing. Combine every statistic, real or jokey, about France's obsession with Jerry Lewis or Germans' with David Hasselhoff and you still don't even get close to how the country devours Moore."

With a new edition of *Downsize This!* in 2003, German publisher Piper planned a tour for Moore through Germany and Austria — *and* commissioned "a special foreword by Moore about the state of the German economy and its foreign policy." Did the man with a high school education have important words to contribute on the subject of the German economy and foreign policy? When Moore published *Downsize This!* in 1996 and began to film his own tour, he could not have known that the Michael Moore media machine had been set permanently in motion. He could not have known his tour would surpass those forty-seven American cities and just keep going.

CHAPTER SEVEN

The Awful Truth of

Working in Television

November 9, 1998. The University of Massachusetts. A man is in the midst of speaking to an audience. Someone in the assembly stands up. He holds aloft an air horn. Its rude noise ripples across the crowd toward the man at the microphone, who is Michael Moore.

Ten years after the completion of *Roger & Me*, Moore had completed an award-winning short sequel, two seasons worth of television, a feature-length fictional film, a best-selling book, and a documentary about his book tour. He had cleared the hill and was entering middle age. His daughter, Natalie Rose, was preparing for university. A decade past pursuing Roger Smith, Moore was even further removed from his little newspaper office at 5005 Lapeer Road. Moore was known across the world in a way he could not have anticipated. The focus was shifting.

Moore could continue to use the formula he had made famous, but not to the same success. He readied himself for a new season of *TV Nation*, to air under another name on the United Kingdom's Channel Four, and in the U.S. and Canada on Bravo cable networks. Unable to employ the title *TV Nation* (still owned by Fox), Moore brought his crusade for truth front and center. "I saw a poster for the movie *The Awful Truth* from back in the '30s," he recalls. "A Cary Grant movie, and I just thought 'I love that title.' It's kind of what we do, so that became the title of the show." The 1937 movie (based on a stage play) depicts Grant and Irene Dunne as the Warriners, a rich couple undergoing divorce. Having already moved on to other socialite lovers, they plot to ruin one another's remarriages. Their main contention is the custody of their beloved prize fox terrier. Having moved on from the Fox Network, perhaps Moore could relate to the little dog. Since *Roger & Me*, the animated logo of his production company, Dog Eat Dog Films, had portrayed a grinning underdog snatching and swallowing in one bite the large growling competition.

In November 1998, Bravo announced its intention to premiere the original twelve-part series in April of the following year. Said Ed Carroll, executive VP and general manager of Bravo, "Michael Moore represents a point of view that's not readily expressed in the media today." Moore was host, creator, and director in this re-envisioned *TV Nation*. Intending to pick up where the first show left off, *The Awful Truth* pointed its cameras at American politicians, corporations, lawyers, and even worked toward policing the police. But long before *The Awful*

Flint, Michigan: a company town. *(© Madison Brown)*

Dr. Martin Luther King Jr. Avenue in Flint. *(© Madison Brown)*

Eagle scout Michael Moore, age fifteen, pledges, "I believe it is my duty to do my best to obey the Scout Oath and Law."

Moore — already a politician at age eighteen.

Always an uncertain future for the *Flint Voice*.

Creating a voice of local opposition.

A house in Burton, Michigan, served as Moore's headquarters for ten years.
(© *Madison Brown*)

Moore and his newspaper crew had to lay down concrete before they could open shop. Their message still remains. (© *Madison Brown*)

Moore addresses a Burton, Michigan, council meeting, as his newspaper grows to become the *Michigan Voice*. *(© 1983 The Flint Journal/Bob Parks. All rights reserved. Reprinted with permission.)*

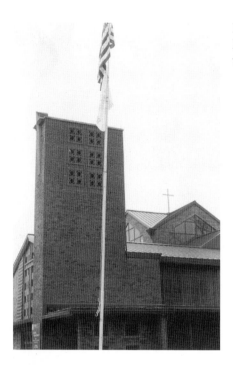

Davison's Catholic church, St. John the Evangelist. Moore reached his first audience through choir. *(© Madison Brown)*

A love of baseball drove Moore from the priesthood.

The Showcase Cinemas in Burton, Michigan, where the *Roger & Me* world premiere was held. *(© Madison Brown)*

Moore addresses the UAW during *Roger & Me* promotion.

A proud papa holds an early copy of his first film.

Truth could air its first episode in its spring, nine o'clock Sunday-night timeslot, the camera would be turned around on Moore.

Alan Edelstein, the man behind that particular camera, was a segment producer of *The Awful Truth* for seven weeks in the summer of '98. During his undergraduate studies, he had begun a film with Peter Friedman called *The Wizard of Strings*, a short documentary which he described as a "student project about an old Vaudeville entertainer." Not exactly student fare, it didn't wrap up until after graduation, then went on to a surprise Oscar nomination in 1985. I interviewed Edelstein in New York City in 2005 for this book. Of his work pre–*Awful Truth*, he said, "We were nominated for an Academy Award and it was hilarious. I worked off and on in film in various capacities, and before being hired by Michael Moore's company, I was working for a small documentary company doing writing and research, and producing PBS kind of stuff." *The Awful Truth* position was the first salaried television job Edelstein had held in many years. Hearing about the show through the grapevine, he applied for a post as a researcher, "a much lower level position than I eventually ended up with." He felt his Academy Award nomination had something to do with the level of the position he was offered, as well as "a sort of comedy test," he admitted he might have done reasonably well on. "I did not come as a fan, nor did I come as a counterspy or as an anti-fan," Edelstein elaborated. "I was not that keen on his work, but I wasn't anti–Michael Moore."

Considering his later conflict with Moore, Edelstein was thoughtful, even gracious, when he spoke about both Moore and the television show, confiding: "I had no real complaints working there. I didn't have run-ins with [Moore] or with anyone else for that matter. As I said, it was my first real TV job and I didn't have much to compare it with. Both myself and the companies that I worked for, the pace is much slower. So it seemed chaotic to me. There were complaints about his inaccessibility, which I guess — to the extent that I was there . . . a little less than two months — I could see, but I didn't have any major complaints of my own. My complaints came after I was gone. . . ." Edelstein continued, "I came into the job knowing he had a bad reputation, but I didn't particularly see the concentration-camp kind of attitude that had been described in the media."

Edelstein did research and groundwork for two episodes of *The Awful Truth* before what was phrased as a "budget problem" resulted in his termination. According to Edelstein, "I never finished either [segment], but I worked on two. One was a William Cohen spoof, the then–Secretary of Defense. The one that was of much more interest to me — which I only did preproduction on — was a piece on the Taliban and televisions. It was basically dropping televisions over Afghanistan. My main interest in life, and for a film I'm working on, is dealing with religion and fundamentalism. So this was much more up my alley. But I didn't get too far with it."

In the Taliban segment that eventually aired, Moore gave a rundown on the political history of Afghanistan (reusing this footage later in *Fahrenheit 9/11*). He visited the New York Taliban offices, questioned them about their religious ban on TV sets, and then presented them with their very own television, bought and paid for through an

Awful Truth–led "TVS-for-the-Taliban" charity drive. The final piece displayed a staged airplane scene where Moore himself delivered the televisions — complete with parachutes — from the sky. A desert scene depicted Afghanis welcoming Moore's idiot-box manna, and gathering around for their first screening of *Roger & Me.*

Though all of Moore's television episodes (from *TV Nation* to *The Awful Truth*) were labor-intensive, the Taliban piece was more demanding, since it involved shooting on foreign soil. For the segment to come off in the way that Moore wanted, it required a great deal of attention. Moore really wanted to shoot it somewhere in South Asia, if not in Afghanistan itself. Said Edelstein, "I had been making calls to find out what it was like to produce something there, so it was not the typical kind of piece." Edelstein also priced out televisions with built-in VCRs, and consulted with aviation experts about how the show could ensure safe landings for their gifts to Afghanistan. Edelstein did feel a pang of concern once when he looked at the board where assignments were posted, and saw that he had only these two assignments in comparison to the other producers, who each had been allotted between four and six. Knowing the Taliban piece was complex, Edelstein dismissed his concern, or rationalized the discrepancy. His dismissal came, he said, "abruptly, suddenly, and really without clear explanation. I was called into the senior producer's office one day and he asked me to shut the door and, you know, immediately I knew there was something irregular going on." Later, Edelstein decided he didn't believe that his dismissal was a standard layoff. He felt he had been fired without explanation, and that Moore was now a prime target for some satire of his own.

The very first episode of *The Awful Truth* depicted a Washington witch-hunt. Following on the heels of President Clinton's affair with Monica Lewinsky, his subsequent impeachment, and the Ken Starr report detailing the President's sex life, *The Awful Truth* sent in a truckload of actors dressed as Puritans to help the people in the White House purge and repent — more affordably. These Puritans were also sent to Starr's home. They chased his car down the street. In another early episode, Moore's brand of humor targeted Lucianne Goldberg, a book agent who persuaded Linda Tripp to record her conversations with Lewinsky on audiotape so they could be used in print. Knowing that an entitlement to privacy is in the U.S. Constitution, Moore asked his studio audience, "What can I do to teach her a lesson about how important our right to privacy is?"

The Awful Truth installed a "LucyCam," playing on the idea of the then-popular "JennyCam." (Given mainstream media coverage on shows such as *Entertainment Tonight*, "JennyCam" was a project by one young woman who wired her dorm-room computer to snap pictures of her studying, sleeping, and yes, occasionally undressing.) Though Lucy's cam was merely a camera trained on Goldberg's apartment window, the images were actually broadcast over a Web site twenty-four hours a day, seven days a week, for a month — and two separate segments and a cam commercial were dedicated to Goldberg on the actual show. An elucidation on the Web site read, "Lucianne does not respect the privacy rights of others. She believes in keeping an eye on persons who are a threat to the country. So do we."

Unfortunately for Moore, so did Edelstein. Feeling he

EMILY SCHULTZ

had been "downsized" unfairly, Edelstein mimicked Moore's tactics of arriving unannounced with a camera in an attempt to get answers. The *New York Times* reported, "During a speech by Mr. Moore at the University of Massachusetts in Amherst, Mr. Edelstein stood up with a camera and a bullhorn, a tool used by Mr. Moore outside the offices of executives. . . . Mr. Edelstein twice showed up with his camera at the office of Mr. Moore's production company on West 57th Street, near 11th Avenue. He filmed some employees but didn't manage to reach Mr. Moore. Later, he took his camera for a few more unsuccessful attempts to engage Mr. Moore at public events outside the office."

At the time of his dismissal Edelstein stated, "I was told that there was a budget crunch, but I don't think that was true. I later learned there were questions about my competence, which no one had ever raised when I was there. So I was angry at the way I was dealt with."

In his interview with me, he recalled the date he confronted Moore at the University of Massachusetts: "It was about two months after I was fired, and I decided for professional reasons to engage in this kind of satirical activity — for the purposes of my own film that I was making. I wouldn't have done anything like this if I hadn't been working on my own film, [where] footage of encounters, or attempted encounters, with him would be useful to me professionally." Edelstein was anxious about confronting the man who had fired him, and Moore was just as uneasy. "He was somewhat flustered initially and then kind of recovered . . ." recounted Edelstein. "But he tried to pretend that I was a plant, that this was part of the show. There was some banter back and forth between me and him, but I didn't pursue it really tenaciously. I sort of slunk away after a minute or two. I'm not sure exactly why. Probably because I was really nervous, and I had done what I needed to do for that night, and I could leave. It's not my style at all. I'm a sort of solitary and nonconfrontational person. So I was doing stuff that was very much out of character and I think that was probably why he was rattled by me, because I don't think he expected this from me."

As of the writing of this book, Edelstein's film was still ongoing. Edelstein called it "an essay or diary film that's been in the works for well over a decade, long before I met Moore or even heard of him — basically a nonbeliever's journey through the world of real belief — true believers Jewish, Christian, and Islamic." Edelstein admitted, "Moore gets worked into the Islamic thing and the Taliban and all that stuff . . . because I met the Taliban people that were based in New York through his show, and that sort of was my *entré* into a whole world, and a whole narrative that I'm trying to make something out of." The only quirk to my interview with Edelstein had to do with his project — he asked if he could interview me and record me at the same time I was recording him, a condition I accepted. How he saw Moore fitting into his own subject matter had to do with his view that Moore's own work can be read as a religious text, and that the role of preacher is part of Moore's character, which is why my interest in Moore fascinated him by association.

"It is not a film in which the main focus is trying to get revenge on Michael Moore or discredit him. Even though he doesn't come off well in the film, it's got a much wider focus than him and his work," Edelstein said. "He's merely my prop, he's not the centerpiece. It's partly confessional, but also journalism. It's a mixture of personal and global issues."

According to the *Washington Post*, after several incidents with Edelstein and his video camera, Moore called Edelstein up and apologized for his treatment at *The Awful Truth*. Edelstein failed to mention this detail during our interview, but did send me the *Post* article containing it. In addition to the incident at the University of Massachusetts, the *Washington Post* reports that he followed Moore to Harlem, where he was shooting a segment of *The Awful Truth*, and also to Chicago where Moore was speaking at the Illinois Institute of Technology.

Moore complained to the police because he believed Edelstein had become a stalker and a threat to his family as well as his other employees. "'If all he was doing was making his little film about me, I wouldn't have cared,' Mr. Moore said," according to the *New York Times*. "'But other people were at risk. This is a disgruntled employee who is a bit off his rocker. Everyone in the office felt there was considerable risk. The women in the office felt frightened for their own safety. Ask them. They'll tell you.'"

Coverage in the *Times* ran a year after Moore's complaint, at which point the *Times* journalist did check with Moore's office and reported thusly, "I *asked* several women, including one recommended by Mr. Moore, and none sounded scared. They said they found Mr. Edelstein a bit obsessive, but otherwise mild-mannered and harmless." The office manager, Kyra Vogt, who was there when Edelstein arrived with his camera, was quoted as saying, "No one was remotely in fear of Alan in any shape or form. . . . Most of us thought the situation was comical. The only person who was paranoid was Michael. He couldn't deal with having someone follow him around."

Edelstein was notified that he would be arrested, but he had the option to surrender himself. On March 8, 1999, he turned himself in to police in Manhattan, arriving at police headquarters with a freelance cameraman, filming. He was taken into custody on charges of harassment and trespassing. At that time, Moore's lawyer Marshall Fishman told the *New York Times* that the situation involved a disgruntled former employee with a personal vendetta against Moore, and that he and Moore were confident the New York Police Department knew how to treat such bullying. They did. At the Midtown North police station, Edelstein was kept for nine hours in a cell. The case was later dropped by the district attorney's office. At a hearing in Manhattan Criminal Court on November 1, 1999, Judge Ellen M. Coin was informed by Assistant District Attorney Erin Koen that the complaining witness did not want to proceed with the case. Edelstein turned around and attempted to sue Moore for malicious prosecution. The *New York Times* piece emerged, and there was a flurry of publicity surrounding Edelstein's suit including the *Washington Post* and also the grocery-store tabloid, *Globe*. *Good Morning America* played the rough footage that Edelstein had shot of Moore.

"Nothing went to court," explained Edelstein. "I was eventually offered a plea bargain which stated if I stayed away from him for six months — him and his family — that the whole thing would just disappear; there'd be no record, etc. Against the advice of my attorney, I declined to take that for two reasons. One: I felt that it was an admission of guilt; and two: I preferred to have my day in court. There was some risk involved, but I felt that the charges were so outrageous that it would be very interesting to see him have to prove some of the things that he said."

Edelstein didn't dwell on the specifics of the case, now six years past. "Like his work," Edelstein commented, "the charges were a mixture of truth and falsehood — as I see his work anyway. There were things in it that were true — like I did go to U Mass, and I did use a megaphone to interrupt him. But there were other things that were really total fabrications, and those were the things that I was interested in him proving. So it was kind of a game of chicken, which I won, and winning it allowed me to sue him. If I had taken the plea bargain it would have been all over."

Edelstein's own suit ended anticlimactically. Though he could not remember the exact details, he believed it might have been dismissed as frivolous.

This was not the first time — nor the only time — that Moore had difficulties with employees or coproducers. In retrospect, as Moore's wife Kathleen Glynn summed it up in a double-feature article on Moore in the *New Yorker*, "along the way, the side of the road was littered with a lot of bad comedy, wasted time and bitter individuals. Past employee grumblings are somewhat pointless.... They exist in a comedy ghetto, one we have pole-vaulted over." Edelstein was only one of the former employees with complaints. There were also Eric Zicklin, a *TV Nation* writer whom the *New Yorker* quoted regarding bad relations with Moore; Chris Kelly, a writer on both *TV Nation* and *Canadian Bacon*; and even John Derevlany, who told me in our interview that, though he felt Glynn was "a very nice lady," he could never "quite figure out what she actually did on *TV Nation*, other than put her name on the credits. I wasn't involved in every single meeting," Derevlany acknowledged, "but I went to plenty of them, and I never really saw her do anything that quite merited the title of producer. I guess her biggest role was managing Michael and his many moods, which, to be honest, is probably a difficult and thankless job."

In Larissa MacFarquhar's lengthy article on Moore in the *New Yorker*, Zicklin was cited as saying, "Michael gave so many people the chance to do jobs that they'd never done before, and that's rare in entertainment. . . . It was incredibly intoxicating for everybody. We came to work thrilled." But the thrill quickly wore off. Though Moore claims he insisted *TV Nation* be a union show and Derevlany confirmed he was paid union scale, Zicklin said he was cautioned alongside another writer that there would not be enough money to pay them both at union rates.

"I can't accept him as a political person," the *New Yorker* quoted Zicklin. "I can't buy into this thing of Michael Moore is on your side — it's like trying to believe that Justin Timberlake is a soulful guy. It's a media product: he's just selling me something."

MacFarquhar's article also quoted crew member Kelly as having had his heart broken by Moore. Though Kelly "thought he was great on the Academy Awards," he said he just could not view Moore's film or read his books. When Moore began writing his column in *The Nation*, Kelly cancelled his subscription. The wounds ran that deep.

Although Moore had been his own media machine pretty much from the age of eighteen, he had initially done it in a city with a population of 200,000. From the time he hit the ground running with *Roger & Me*, Moore had had no real break from national attention. When he hadn't been in the media's eye, he created his own press, as he did with *The Big One*, turning his own book tour into a feature film — essentially a vehicle for self-promotion. Some might suggest that there were more words in the film than in the book. Where was the line between Michael Moore and the Michael Moore industry? In addition to directing a team of fifty full-time staff, plus freelancers, on *The Awful Truth*, there was the upkeep of his Web site, the diaristic E-mail missives going out regularly to "Mike's Militia," and, as if that wasn't enough, Moore's next feature film, *Bowling for Columbine*, was already underway. While there were problems with *The Awful Truth* financially — the team tearing through the budget with the first few episodes, then stretching to make ends meet — the cheapness of the pranks did not come entirely from petty cash (or lack thereof). In the second season, the show's humor became increasingly morbid, as if *Columbine* had laid a tombstone atop Moore's sense of comedy.

Moore did issue apologies to Kelly, and to former correspondent Merrill Markoe, saying, "I reached a point, a place in my life where I didn't see myself as a perfect person, and I wanted to apologize for anything I've done or said to people." He also acknowledged, "This is not the easiest type of show to do. It takes a lot out of all of us." Without Glynn, whom he considered the most important person on the show, Moore said he didn't know how he or the cast would have gotten through it.

In spite of conflicts in the world of television, it was during *The Awful Truth* years that Moore began building the team he would continue to work with. Creative consultant Jay Martel was one of these writers/producers, and stuck by Moore through *TV Nation*, *The Awful Truth*, *Bowling for Columbine*, and *Fahrenheit 9/11*. His role on *The Awful Truth* was a significant one, covering a lot of the hard-hitting stories, such as the Gulf War Fun Run, a charity race in which former soldiers suffering from Gulf War Syndrome ran (or, more accurately, walked very slowly or wheelchair-rolled) to raise funds to help with their own war-related medical expenses, unacknowledged by the U.S. government.

Correspondent Karen Duffy also supported Moore on both shows — and beyond. She sees the complaints brought against Moore as petty, saying, "I think they're a bunch of girls and they should take off their skirts and stop crying . . . It's TV! When you're putting out a weekly show, you're under a lot of pressure, but I've worked with [Michael] for five years, and I've never seen him blow up." Duffy was also quoted in the *New Yorker* as saying, "I've never done anything I've been more proud of than working with Michael Moore. I just hate the way the left is constantly cannibalizing itself."

Thankfully for Moore (and for Duffy, who was a frequent presence on the show), the press had better things to say about his television work than some of his ex-employees did. In spite of the show's opener — in which an announcer read, "By the end of the millennium five men controlled the media," while the floating heads of Rupert Murdoch, Michael Eisner, Ted Turner, Sumner Redstone, and Bill Gates surrounded a whirling globe — the print media was fair to Moore. Though *The Awful Truth* recycled the formula — and often the content — of its previous incarnation, it was still considered wildly refreshing.

Emerging on Bravo, the first episodes of *The Awful Truth* were running alongside other irreverent cable programs, such as *The Tom Green Show* and *Celebrity Deathmatch*. *Celebrity Death-match*, a claymation MTV creation, depicted different celebrity animé each week in a wrestling ring. The matches, which faced-off nonathletic personalities (such as movie directors Martin Scorsese and Oliver Stone), were given narrative and in-jokes using a variety of filmic techniques — as well as a wide array of blood-and-guts effects as the characters decapitated one another claymation-style. In the post–*South Park* world, it was now permissible for fecal matter to bounce out of the toilet and become an animated character. The political correctness that had dominated the early '90s was dying as many deaths as the shack-dwelling "Kenny McCormick" — Matt Stone and Trey Parker's icon for the poor.

The change from *TV Nation* to *The Awful Truth* brought with it a new echelon of confrontation, and a raised level of accepted cruelty. While *The Awful Truth* was staging a pre-mortis funeral outside of Humana, an H.M.O. company refusing to provide coverage for a Florida man in need of a heart transplant, Canadian comedian Tom Green was rubbing "dog poo" on a microphone before sticking it in the faces of random individuals on the street whom he approached for interview. Green was riding a cow into a grocery store, then getting underneath it to suck on its udder. As Caryn James acknowledged in the *New York Times*, "the major networks would consider these shows subversive, though in many respects they provide a better measure of social attitudes than the cautious networks ever could. . . . When they are willfully rude, as so many are, they reflect the cultural grittiness that is given a cosmetic gloss by the network entertainment machines."

While acknowledging that some *Awful Truth* segments were spent showing Moore being predictably shut out by public relations people, the *Times* conceded that "the show energetically reflects the lunacy of living in a corporate culture. What celebrities are to *Deathmatch*, big-money executives are to *The Awful Truth*."

The Emmy nominations would not come as they did with *TV Nation*, but with its first nine episodes, *The Awful Truth* did receive a Hugh M. Hefner First Amendment Award in the Arts and Entertainment category. The Playboy Foundation insisted, "with humor and satire, the show educates the public about issues critical to preserving First Amendment rights. Using the guerilla tactics he documented in *Roger & Me*, Moore satirizes, badgers, and pokes fun at the people who are the news. He continuously and relentlessly battles censorship to express his viewpoints regarding a wide range of social issues in the United States." This was an award usually given to a lowly *liberal*, Moore's shibboleth, and not professed a leftist — a distinction Moore still consistently points out regarding himself.

The Awful Truth's first season was, in many ways, more catch-as-you-can than its predecessor had been. Moore wasn't battling the Klan this time around, but he was able to amass a pink RV full of discoing gay men and women, call it the "Sodomobile," and drive it to every state that made it illegal to be gay. On *TV Nation*, Moore had attempted to raise gay issues by confronting the high school of the nephew of Pastor Fred Phelps, who con-

EMILY SCHULTZ

doned the picketing of funerals of AIDS victims. This time, Moore and the members of the Sodomobile took on the pastor himself. Phelps' response? "You guys are heading straight to hell in a faggot's handbasket."

Jostling among other headstrong comedy shows on cable, *The Awful Truth* had a studio audience made up more of thirtysomethings than the show's youthful pranks might suggest. Yet a portable mosh pit is what would land the show in the national news — and in the 2000 presidential debates. During the 2000 election primaries, *The Awful Truth* was searching for a new way to pick a president. Their solution? Put the candidates in the mosh pit! According to Moore, the idea came from the bottom up: "Some of our best ideas have come from the viewers and it's alleged that we actually pay for these ideas, but I've never seen a check go out, so I'm not sure about that." Just before the Iowa Caucus in January 2000, *The Awful Truth* crew headed to Des Moines. They picked up a truckload of high school students, and to the tune of "Guerrilla Radio" by Rage Against the Machine — on a school day no less — drove them to Republican candidate Gary Bauer's election headquarters. Moore can no longer remember if the show even had insurance to put the disorderly kids on the moving truck. In his DVD commentary, he wonders if their parents could have sued. Luckily, no one did fall off the truck. The teenagers rowdily jumped for warmth on the flatbed, penned in only by orange plastic snow fencing. Shortly after arriving, two Des Moines police officers arrived to tell Moore that the kids were being too loud, and were therefore disturbing the peace. Even if they stopped yelling, the officer told Moore, they were still trespassing. For Moore, the word "trespassing" was a red flag. He knew that whenever police use this word, it's time to leave. The mosh pit for Democracy kept moving, and fast.

When Moore attempted to convince future president and nemesis George W. Bush to join him outside for some mosh action, Bush replied, "Behave yourself, will you. Go find real work!" In response, Michael phoned his own father and asked if he had an oil company he could give him to run, or maybe a major league baseball team. All unplanned, according to Moore. His father Frank's response? "Uh, say that again?"

The segment found its finisher with Alan Keyes and his campaign people. Without much prompting, Chris Jones, Keyes' National Campaign Director, agreed to bodysurf the teen pit. He took his suit jacket off in minus 10 weather, and dove right in. Moore couldn't believe it: "When this happened I just thought, 'Well, okay, we've got the piece now. This is about as good as it's going to get.'" But Keyes' young daughter also convinced her father to surf the Mosh Pit for Democracy. Keyes dropped backwards, arms spread, Jesus-like, into the cheering teen crowd. "This is a presidential candidate — running for President of the United States," Moore recalled. "Unbelievable. At that moment I am just freaking out. I cannot believe that this is happening . . . I'm going, 'Oh boy, what are we doing on Bravo with this? This is too good.'"

A photograph of Keyes holding up one of his signs while he himself was borne aloft wound up, to quote Moore, "in every newspaper across the country. We were on every news show that night." Jay Leno, CNN, CNBC, Conan O'Brien, and others blurbed it on their shows. Said Gail Collins of the *New York Times* on CNN's *The*

World Today, "I'm sorry, the mosh pit was so great that nothing else conceivably could have [competed]."

During the debates, Keyes was critiqued for the act, yet turned it to his favor, using the mosh pit as a metaphor for how the American people will hold one another up. "Admittedly I was willing to fall into the mosh pit," Keyes countered. "You know why I did that? Because I think that exemplifies the kind of trust in people that is the heart and soul of the Keyes campaign." For a fringe candidate, Keyes ranked a surprising third in the debates — though by the end of the race, the American public did not bear him up as their presidential candidate. In *The Awful Truth* commentary, flabbergasted by his own antics, Moore burst out, "Folks, do you understand? Yeah, this is a *presidential* debate, okay. They're *debating* the mosh pit. Hello?"

Gail Collins attempted to make more sense of the mosh pit scandal. "There is, believe it or not, a larger issue at work here," she wrote in the *New York Times*. "All the candidates for president have been promising to bring decorum back to the White House. But they're campaigning in an age when politicians are forced to compete with entertainment celebrities for TV time and magazine covers, and the temptation to do something peculiar to get attention keeps expanding." Collins continued bitingly, "The Democrats are about to say goodbye to a president who discussed his underwear preferences on MTV, and the Republicans are looking for a successor to the guy now starring in TV ads about erectile dysfunction."

With Alan Keyes in the portable mosh pit, *The Awful Truth* was front-page news. But why spend it all in one place? Moore had just jumped onboard the production of a music video for the band Rage Against the Machine, when he got the call telling him *The Awful Truth* was being discussed in the presidential debate. Rage Against the Machine had emerged from the Los Angeles underground music scene in 1992 with a raw sound that meshed punk, hip-hop, and thrash. Their uncensored lyrics encouraged revolt against corporate America, government oppression, and the status quo in general. Teaming up with the popular Porno for Pyros, and joining the second and third Lollapalooza tours, Rage's unexpected hits, "Bullet in the Head" and "Killing in the Name," wound up pounding from car stereos and shrieking across college campuses throughout 1993. In Philadelphia at Lollapalooza III, Rage Against the Machine staged a silent protest against censorship — in the nude. For fifteen minutes they stood onstage naked without singing or playing a note. Their mouths were duct-taped, and each band member wore a scrawled letter on his chest, spelling out "P-M-R-C," the moral watchdogs of the music industry. Rage Against the Machine became well known for their outsider status, playing anti-Nazi League concerts, and Rock for Choice abortion rights concerts, as well as touring in 1993 with pothead hip-hoppers Cypress Hill.

For their 1999 album, *The Battle of Los Angeles*, the band wanted Moore to direct their video. The song was "Sleep Now in the Fire," and Moore wanted to "shoot this in the belly of the beast." He set up on the steps of the Federal Building, while the band erected their equipment right in front of the New York Stock Exchange. Before a crowd of approximately 300 fans, the band fired up their instruments and ran through "Sleep Now . . ." six times. At that point, the police arrived and ordered the impromptu concert to come to a close. "Before we had a chance to stop, four officers jumped me and put me in one of those police locks like you see on that excellent and informative show *Cops*," Moore claimed. "One tried to break my arm, the other put a chokehold on my neck. In all my years of shooting in New York, I have never had this happen, and all I could think of was, well, I just hope it's a new plunger."

The throng took to the official intrusion less well than Moore: they proceeded to jump police barricades and rush for the doors of the Stock Exchange. A formerly peaceful crowd had now become a riot situation. Before the young people could breach the Stock Exchange, a set of titanium gates crashed down, protecting the next set of double doors. The New York Stock Exchange closed a full two hours early this day — a highly unusual event. During that same time, social conservative Gary Bauer was flubbing the band's name in the debates. With unintended irony, he called them "The Machine Rages On."

The Awful Truth did put together an Alan Keyes endorsement that played during the second season's third episode. It began with a headshot of Keyes and the American National Anthem. At the end, it segued into the mosh pit footage: "Before you decide to vote for Alan Keyes, there's a few things you should know. Alan Keyes is against a woman's right to choose. Alan Keyes is against affordable health care. Alan Keyes is pro-censorship, anti-gay, and insists on being called Ambassador even though he's really just a radio talk show host." The question the commercial raised was why would *The Awful Truth* ask its audience to vote for Alan Keyes. The answer was obvious: because he had dared to enter the mosh pit.

The Keyes scandal was one of the glory moments of

The Awful Truth's second season. Unfortunately, the show, like Keyes, was only held aloft for a few moments — then it was straight down. A scaled-back budget — in combination with Moore and Martel's divided energies between the show and the new film — led to new problems and concessions. Moore's stand-up schtick in front of a studio audience was stripped between seasons one and two. Moore now stood alone at night with a microphone in the middle of Times Square. He would query random passersby, and urge them to look deep into the camera as he unveiled the newest segment of *Truth*. Even the opening musical montage was different, relying on Beethoven because it cost nothing to use. Between convertible rentals (for Martel to get to Florida to cheer Jeb Bush's state executions as if they were football games) and airfares (for Moore to activist jet-set between Minnesota and the state capitol on behalf of deportation-threatened Mexican workers), the budget was eaten up in just a few episodes. Second season stunts dragged on, or relied on pranks that required few props. Moore took ideas he had run in his *Michigan Voice* days, such as the automobile industry's reliance on concentration camp labor, and rescripted them for television. Moore sent in Sal Piro, *The Awful Truth* Bill Collector, a hired thug, to get some straight talk out of BMW's headquarters in New Jersey. When Piro met with silence, he took out his trusty crowbar and introduced it to a BMW — one that had been hired from a local rental office. For the price of a broken window, *The Awful Truth* had a show.

Consider "Pie the Poor," a segment in which correspondent Duffy organizes teams of willing millionaires to compete against one another in the humiliating of actual homeless people and folks of modest wages. Culled from Wall Street during happy hour, these necktied gentlemen were divided into Team Dow and Team Nasdaq. They took turns throwing cream pies into faces, and baseballs at a tank in a game of "Dunk the Homeless." The supposedly homeless subject, "Frank," who was found in Times Square and paid for his appearance on the program, looked none too happy. "Pin the Tail on the Illegal Alien" was another nasty little game, in which the faces of subjects "Maria" and "Claudio" were blurred out. In his commentary, Moore admits the obvious, that it's "pretty dark." The millionaires were more than willing to perform, and Moore claims that by the end of the night, some of them understood the satire.

A similar sketch, "Dixie Flag Night," appeared on episode seven. As an interlude to the longer segments, random African Americans in Times Square faced the camera and informed the audience how many hours they were working (lots), how much money they were making (little), and what benefits they received (none). Then they held up their hands in fake cuffs and said, "Take me back to the plantation."

On episode ten, *The Awful Truth* crew decided to "Track the Homeless." Correspondent Duffy visited Cathy Choquette, a woman who actually lived in Manhattan Mini Storage, because it was safer and cleaner than the streets. Later in the show, correspondent Martel pretended to ship the homeless overseas, fitting a young black woman into a crate, tossing in Styrofoam chips for softness — and a couple of sandwiches, just in case. Correspondent Hamper helped fit the homeless into the trunks of parked cars, as well as into empty garbage cans.

One of the most disturbing second-season segments was a response to the New York City police shooting of Amadou "Ahmed" Diallo. On February 4, 1999, at approximately 12:45 a.m., Diallo was shot forty-one times by four plainclothes police officers in the vestibule of the apartment building where he lived in the Bronx. A West African immigrant from the French-speaking country of Guinea, Diallo was a devoted Muslim who had been in New York since 1996 and had no criminal record. The officers, all white, were searching that night for a serial rapist. No weapons were found on Diallo's body or at the scene, though his wallet and his pager were nearby. Two of the officers fired sixteen times each, the other two officers, four and five times each. Three of the four officers had records of shootings; two of these shootings were resolved, the third still under investigation. Nineteen of the bullets struck Diallo, who died of gunshot wounds to his torso.

New York's then-mayor Rudolph Giuliani urged that no one jump to conclusions. "It's obviously troubling to both the police commissioner and myself that forty-one shots were fired," he said on Court TV, but when questioned he would not come up with a situation that might warrant that number of shots to be fired. Black leaders — including the Reverend Al Sharpton, and President of the United African Congress, Sidique Wai — called for a federal investigation.

The officers walked. Within twenty-four hours of the officers' release, *The Awful Truth* set up a table in Harlem. It was a Saturday morning, and the entire crew was present. Moore led the segment as the team exchanged the dark wallets of black citizens for neon orange wallets that were less likely to be mistaken for guns by police. Tensions were high in Harlem that particular day. "Some people, I have to admit, on the crew were a little nervous about doing this," Moore recalled, "But we had . . . quite a positive response from people there in Harlem and they completely got wha t we were trying to do. Everyone . . . people walking by wanted to participate in this." In Florida, Jerome Richardson had been shot while holding a set of house keys; seventeen-year-old Andre Burgess had been shot while holding a Three Musketeers chocolate bar. *The Awful Truth* spray-painted keys and chocolate-bar wrappers bright safety orange so that these objects — in the hands of black Americans — would not instantly transform into weapons. *The Awful Truth* also handed out costume bullet wounds, so black men could pretend they had already been shot — the idea being that if they were already dead, the police would leave them alone. Another black man was provided with garbage-bag camouflage, so whenever police came near he could duck under it, blending seamlessly into the urban landscape.

But did the satire just extend the idea that African-American life is cheap, rather than simply drawing attention to these very real stereotypes? Happy music played in the background as an entire street full of black Americans, including toddlers, raised their arms "don't shoot"–style above their heads while going about their days — but happy music could not make for happy television or a happy country. The spark of rebellion that was present in *TV Nation*, coupled with a Christian kind of do-unto-others moral guarding, was not only lacking from *The Awful Truth*, it was replaced with a deep, gaping cynicism. Audiences know, watching the piece, that no solution will emerge, that white officers will continue to see guns where there are only cell phones. At the same time, on a day that could have been as explosive as the L.A. riots, hundreds of black Americans exchanged their wallets instead. A dump truck's worth of good leather wallets were discarded, symbolically delivered to New York's 32nd precinct.

It is this duality of cynicism and ethics that defines the character of Michael Moore. When the English *Guardian* interviewed him a couple of years after *The Awful Truth* had come to an end, Moore offered a clearer portrait of his emotional take on the world around him than he did during the show. Questioned about his methods for keeping his spirits up, and how he managed to forge onward, Moore responded: "Jeez, I think I'm right. The things I believe in, I believe strongly enough in them and I think I'm right. When I'm wrong, then I change my mind and I'm right again. I try to keep my sense of humour. . . ." Moore credited his ability to continue to have faith, saying, "Maybe there's something in that Catholic upbringing — where all things seem unattainable, everything is insurmountable, the odds are always against you. I'm the person in the lifeboat, where if the lifeboat was full of holes and going down and all there was was a Dixie cup, I'd be the one still bailing the water . . ."

But when the same question was rephrased specifically to pertain to hope for the American political system, Moore admitted, "Maybe what I'm saying is that maybe I'm just crazy. That maybe there isn't any hope for the United States. We've had our moment, we had a chance to do great things with it. We started out by doing a few good things but then we blew it."

In his 1988 release, "Tower of Song," Leonard Cohen

sang about the rich having their television channels in the bedrooms of the poor. Continually Moore stressed the realness of the people on *The Awful Truth* and their situations, as he has on most of his projects. Though most fictional television series to some extent rely on poor characters to move plot, these series always use actors to play the poor. The question we need to ask is why watching fiction happen in a nonfictional setting frightens us. When we understand this, we will understand Michael Moore as a cultural phenomenon. Whether "real" or not, Moore's TV segments were also constructs, carefully thought out or written — then cast and coordinated — by Moore, Duffy, and a full television team, where casting sessions for "Pie the Poor" contests amounted to someone running to a series of upscale bars at New York Stock Exchange quitting time.

I asked Moore's foil Edelstein, as a fellow documentarian, how he felt about Moore's documentary style. "I'm not the right person to ask about that, just because I have had such a long and weird time with him," he qualified. At the same time he said, "My main problem is that . . . I think he's a deeply dishonest person and filmmaker. As a former print journalist, a documentarian, he claims to be beholden to the facts and truth and . . . I think that falls by the wayside in his work. You know, so much of your opinion of his stuff is based on your take on him, and whether you like him as a character."

CHAPTER EIGHT

Gun Crazy

Bowling for Success

One day [Moore and the crew] wanted to know if Hitler ever went bowling.

— *Michael Moore's researcher*

Calling what Moore did "toiling in television" might be an exaggeration, as his work for the small screen gave Moore success and credibility beyond his *Roger & Me* audience. But it was not the place Moore had wanted to spend the better part of the 1990s. While his development pile showed his desire to break out of television and into mainstream film, the leap still eluded him. In spite of a bestselling book, the failure of *Canadian Bacon* to find a place in the multiplexes and the undersized reception for *The Big One* must have needled Moore. To continue in television would be like being one of those Flint guys stuck on the line — bored, but in love with the easy money.

While Channel Four had been an eager booster of Moore's work and *The Awful Truth* for its first season, that support started to wane both financially and in scheduling. As Moore had always done in the past, he cured any creative malaise he might have had by throwing himself into several more projects. It was at *The Awful Truth* offices on Tuesday, April 20, 1999 that Moore found his next film project *Bowling for Columbine* thrust upon him.

The day of the tragedy at Columbine High School, Moore arrived at work to find his crew members gathered around the television, like most Americans were, watching events unfold in Colorado. "The image that really — really — just assaulted me was the one where [clears throat] the kids were all told to put their hands up, and all told to line up against the wall with their hands up behind their heads," Moore later told a live audience in Littleton. "In other words, you are *all* suspect. You are *all* [the] potential murderer. You will *all* come out with your hands up and keep them up. I just felt that day I had to do something . . . I've thought about this issue, about what a violent country we are, for a long time."

As *The Awful Truth* was being punted into a late-night nowhere timeslot in the U.K., Moore slowly soured on the whole television thing. It became his day job, while he continued do his real work — *Bowling for Columbine*, his personal response to that year's great domestic tragedy. Armed with an office for his TV production, he kept a threadbare crew of friends and more than a dozen unpaid (though when financing came later, paid) interns

— including his daughter Natalie Rose — researching, filming, and editing what would become Moore's return to water-cooler discussions the world over.

Outside of Denver, the bedroom community known as Littleton, Colorado — where Columbine High School was located — had seen a multitude of torrid media reports regarding the massacre that occurred there on April 20, 1999, the 110th anniversary of Adolf Hitler's birth. Unlike other tragedies occurring in the wired world, the Columbine incident marked the first time news officials were hooked into the inside of a tragedy while it was still occurring. Cell-phoned reports from students hiding from the gunmen were telecast even before the area had been evacuated. America literally huddled in fear with its youth, waiting for answers.

Shortly after 11 a.m., two senior students, Dylan Klebold and Eric Harris entered Columbine High School, from which they were scheduled to graduate in only a few weeks. In the cafeteria, which housed approximately 500 lunching students, they deposited two twenty-pound propane bombs disguised in duffel bags. Making their way back out of the school, they waited for their bombs to go off. Had things gone according to their plan, nearly everyone in the cafeteria would have been killed. As detailed over the previous year in Harris's occasional journal, the boys' original plan was to wait outside and shoot only as their classmates fled school. But when the boys' homemade bombs refused to go off, they entered the school again, only minutes later, armed with four different types of guns and numerous pipe bombs.

As the first couple of Columbine students were killed, many heard the gunshots but attributed them to a graduation prank. Longtime teacher and coach Dave Sanders realized what was going on, rushed into the school and shouted out warnings, enabling teachers and janitors to shepherd students immediately to safety. Sanders continued through the school, warning students out of harm's way, until he himself was wounded by Klebold and Harris. He was pulled into a classroom, where hiding students attempted to staunch Sanders' chest wound until he expired three hours later, just after the SWAT teams reached him. Though the SWAT teams had been quick to arrive on the scene, along with local police, they were fired at through windows by the boys. When SWAT members did enter the school at noon, they first set to diffusing bombs rather than attempting to secure the area or remove students from the school, which would not happen until after 2:30 in the afternoon.

By noon, parents were aware of what was happening, and awaited their children at Leawood Elementary School, where students who had made it out were being shuttled. Other parents flocked to Columbine High itself, and remained behind police tape. Within their first hour in the high school, Klebold and Harris had fired 188 rounds of ammunition and thrown 76 bombs, before turning their weapons upon themselves. Though they'd had a hit list, none of those killed were on it. At the end of the day, twenty-five people were injured, three of whom were in critical condition, and fifteen people were dead — twelve students, one teacher, and the two murderers. According to a follow-up article published six months after Columbine in *Salon*, a key source said, "we can tell you why they did it, because they tell us why they're going to do it. . . . They did it because they were consumed with hate." Division Chief John Kiekbusch, the ranking officer overseeing the case, confirmed this source, saying, "they hated everybody and everything."

These were not the statements appearing in the news on that day, however. Perhaps fueled by the accounts given by traumatized high school students, the media reports immediately searched for simple rumor-style solutions, the most prevalent depicting a "Trench Coat Mafia" associated with Goth music and destruction (though neither Klebold or Harris dressed in the Goth style). Other explanations for the killing spree were racism (though only one of the murdered students was black), an anti-Christian agenda (though only one girl was asked if she believed in God), and a hatred of jocks (though Harris himself was a soccer player, and most of the violence took place in the library, not the gym). Media also attributed a larger percentage of the killings and the shots to Harris, playing up Klebold's passive nature, and constructing a leader-and-follower dynamic between the boys. But when the investigation team closed their case, they reported nearly equal involvement in the destruction. America wanted answers — beyond the ambiguous notion of an unbiased, all-encompassing hate — and it still does.

Above and beyond the simple tragedy of the event, the Columbine school killings became, in the media-swollen world of 1999, whatever pundits and commentators wanted them to be. For many, the attack was a sign of youth corrupted by permissive culture and a lack of traditional values. For others, it was the evidence that the American way of life was producing emotionless psychopaths proportional to its material wealth, invoking Emma Goldman's sangfroid aphorism that "a society gets every criminal it deserves."

For Moore, this terrible event was not just a central theme to build his film around — a film that would grow to encompass broad indictments of violence in America and America's role in violence across the world — but, like his most successful work, the subject matter was personal. Flint was still Moore's mirror for interpreting the effects of politics and, much to the chagrin of his critics, this was where Moore excelled. By capturing (or "selecting," a detractor might say) how everyday America is affected by the ambiguity of domestic and foreign policies, Moore was able to pull such tangles out of the world of abstraction. Columbine shooter Harris had lived in Oscoda, Michigan, while his father was stationed at a military base there. Oscoda is located in northern Michigan, and Moore had spent so long defining his personality by the state at large, he was deeply affected by this fact.

Another Michigan connection would emerge unexpectedly during the filming. Just after Moore started *Bowling for Columbine*, on February 29, 2000, Flint became home to the youngest school shooter in U.S. history when six-year-old Kayla Rowland was shot and killed by a classmate at Buell Elementary, an urban school in the Flint-Beecher school district, and the poorest in Genessee County. Though Moore would cover the incident in *Bowling for Columbine*, this was also a personal setback for him, as Buell was the very school where Moore's and Phil Knight of Nike's $20,000 Flint school contribution had gone after they parted ways in *The Big One*. In an open letter on his Weblog, Moore described the Buell area as "Flint's dump." "It is where you go when you have nothing left to your name. 60% black, 40% white. No municipality in Genesee

County wants to govern Beecher, so it exists as a No Man's Land on the northern city limits of Flint." And the school's district of Beecher was personal to Moore for other reasons. "It covers a small portion of two different townships (one of which is where my wife Kathleen is from). But folks, when you hear the word 'township' used in the case of Beecher, those of us from Flint mean it in the way the word was used in South Africa."

It was grim luck, and Moore would continue to find history unfolding around his film. Though the Flint community came together and rallied around Buell Elementary, including donations of playground equipment and government grants to the township for policing and gun-control efforts, Buell Elementary closed its doors in 2002, before *Bowling for Columbine* saw wide release. The teacher depicted in Moore's movie moved elsewhere; the principal and superintendent retired. Former Genesee County prosecutor Arthur Busch, who handled the case, seconded Moore's opinion of the township, telling the Associated Press that parents who lived there faced some of the state's highest unemployment rates, that the majority of kids were eligible for free or reduced-price lunches, and that delinquency and neglect cases were still straining the system in 2005. "The ingredients that created this scenario still exist: child poverty, drugs, all that misery that comes with poverty," Busch said.

The shooting of Kayla Rowland inspired Moore to seek out American actor and National Rifle Association spokesman, Charlton Heston. Moore felt Heston, who had spoken at gun rallies in both Denver and Flint just after the two tragedies, had been insensitive to these communities. Attempting to schedule an interview with the actor through normal channels, Moore was unsuccessful. In preparation for the interview, Moore became a lifetime member of the NRA. He hoped his card-carrying status would help convince Heston and others he wasn't out to get them, although in truth, his original plan was a little trickier. Back in Moore's Boy Scout days, he had been a junior member of the NRA, but after the Columbine massacre he decided to become a lifetime member. "My first thought after Columbine was to run against Charlton Heston for the presidency of the NRA. You have to be a lifetime member to be able to do that, so I had to pay $750 . . . to join," Moore told *The Guardian.* "My plan was to get 5000 Americans to join for the lowest basic membership and vote for me so that I'd win and dismantle the organization. Unfortunately . . . that's just too much work for me," Moore confessed. "So instead I made this movie. But I'm still a lifetime member, until they excommunicate me . . . which is not far off, from what I hear."

Moore may not remain in the NRA, but he did nail that interview with Heston. On the crew's last day in Hollywood, just as the van was to head to the airport, they decided to make one last-ditch effort to get their interview: they purchased a star map.

"So I ring the buzzer," said Moore. "And out of that little box came the voice of Moses. 'Yes?' And I'm going, 'Oh my God, What am I gonna do?' And then he told me, come back tomorrow morning, and he'd give me the interview. And he did." In his late seventies at the time of the interview, Heston almost didn't make his appearance in the film, as Moore himself wavered on including the footage. He felt Heston's age, very apparent in the footage, particularly since he was recovering from hip surgery, would skewer audience reaction. In the end, most of the interview was included: Heston's remarks regarding race and violence in America, and Heston turning his back on Moore — walking away from the offered photograph of Flint's youngest gun fatality, Kayla Rowland. According to Moore, even before the editing room, it was a scene that almost wasn't.

"I did become afraid after the interview, after you see me walk out the driveway. . . . You don't see what happens after that 'cause we went to credits, but we got to the gate and they wouldn't let me out," said Moore in interview during the Cannes festival. "And I thought, well, they're calling people to come and take our film from us, and to beat me up." Moore removed the footage from the camera, and threw it over top of the gate to some of his crew who had been waiting outside in case of emergency. Though nothing untoward happened, Moore claims he told the crew, "Get in the car and just drive the hell out of here. You know, we'll take our licks, but at least we'll have the film."

Though some viewers felt the scene was emotionally exploitive, Moore said, in retrospect, "I don't know why anybody would feel sorry for a guy who leads the most powerful lobby group in the U.S., and whose sole purpose is to make sure people can have as many guns as they want to have and fire as many bullets as the guns can possibly fire. . . . These people are insane, and they have to be stopped," he added. "And the majority of Americans, according to every poll, want gun control. . . ."

In addition to the Heston exchange; interviews with Buell Elementary principal Jimmie Hughes; detectives and townspeople of Littleton; as well as the much-blamed singer Marilyn Manson (of whom Klebold and Harris were reportedly fans); *Bowling for Columbine*, like *Roger & Me*, would rely on the expert editing of archival footage, voice-over, and original footage. Responsible for bringing all this together, with funding equal to four episodes of *TV Nation*, were the interns who worked primarily for the experience. Production ran smoothly, and most described it as a learning experience. One researcher recalled that Moore made the group watch *The Battle of Algiers*, Gillo Pontecorvo's 1965 sparely styled documentary-like chronicle of the Algerian Revolution. Technically a fictional film, Ponte-corvo's rehash cast the actual leaders of the revolution, so the line between fiction and reality blurred. The film's veracity is so well-regarded that it infamously found itself being screened by the Pentagon in 2004 to prepare leaders for what a street battle might entail in an Arabic country. This kind of "performance of truth" is clearly not far from Moore's intentions with his own work.

As Alan Edelstein, former–*Awful Truth* employee, said, "I look at [Moore] basically as a failed priest. He went to seminary and was thrown out — you know, again, according to him — a year later. But he was a very sincere and interested Catholic. I see certain aspects of his work are preachy in a way that I associate with someone who needs a replacement for religion. It's of interest to me that he's still very connected to the church." In promotional commentary with the DVD version of *Bowling for Columbine*, an intern echoed Edelstein's assessment by calling Moore "Father Mike," describing Moore's ability to make subjects feel at ease and "submit to the camera."

Once the film saw release, critics attacked this fiction/

documentary dichotomy, as they had with *Roger & Me*, claiming in particular that the opening scene — in which Moore opens a bank account and walks out the same day with a shotgun — was staged. When Andrew Collins of the *Guardian* interviewed Moore at the London Film Festival, he questioned Moore about notions of authorship.

"So this is an author piece," Collins said. "It's the best way to describe the films that you make — you're in them, you write the text that goes into them and you go out to prove or disprove something you think needs proving or publicising. But there's a fine line, isn't there?"

Amid self-deprecating comments regarding his own ego, Moore said, "I exist in my films as a stand-in for the audience." At the same time, like the audience, Moore found certain scenes too emotional to watch. Both he and Glynn found themselves in tears watching the movie for the hundredth time when it came to the portions dealing with Rowland's death.

Though the visual and audio punch of *Bowling for Columbine* would strain the budget, one music track was given to the production for next to nothing — the Beatles' "Happiness Is a Warm Gun." Notoriously, the Beatles and their estates have never allow their recordings to be used in films, but Yoko Ono, who lost John Lennon to Mark Chapman's gunfire in 1981, made sure her husband's composition was available to Moore. "We got a good deal on it, too," Glynn told the press. The song is set to a fascinating, but emotionally devastating, series of images culled from the news media, including politician Bud Dwyer's on-air suicide during a press conference in 1987, as well as footage of the 1993 shooting of Maritza Martin Munoz by her estranged husband, a killing that took place during a live newscast. The camera did not stop once as Emilio Munoz fired fourteen rounds. To provide this assault on the senses, the *Bowling for Columbine* crew had to spend a full month of editing on this sequence alone.

Also used to harrowing effect was surveillance footage from Columbine High School. Backtracked by audio from 911 calls (including a chilling statement from a panicking teen trapped inside the school — that she had spoken to Fox News, but not the police yet), the black-and-white footage was rarely seen in its entirety, and was obtained by Moore only through the Freedom of Information Act. For Moore, the footage of heavily armed teenagers from a wealthy suburb walking calmly through their high school while throwing bombs and stopping for a sip from a soda left at a table, would say more than he ever could about violence in American society.

At the same time as Moore was in the early stages with *Bowling for Columbine*, another maverick filmmaker was looking at the killings and trying to make sense of them through his art. Gus Van Sant had, like Moore, come into the mainstream spotlight from the margins at the start of the '90s. The son of a traveling salesman, Van Sant directed *Drugstore Cowboy*, like *Roger & Me*, a breakout hit of 1989 that seemed to come from nowhere. Van Sant would go on to make subtly subversive movies for mainstream audiences, exploring hustlers and queer sexuality in *My Own Private Idaho*, and the media and obsession with fame in *To Die For*. Like Moore, Van Sant would also share his wealth, supporting cutting edge filmmakers such as Nina Menkes.

In 1999, Van Sant went to HBO looking for funding for a documentary on the Columbine shootings. Presciently,

HBO said no to his proposal, but were willing to provide support for a *fictional* film based loosely on the events. HBO head Colin Callendar told Van Sant that the "bombardment of violent images from twenty-four-hour news operations are increasingly difficult to decipher," and that creating a fictional film would do the subject more justice. After regrouping, Van Sant started his project again as a narrative film — using real teenagers improvising without a written script. When Van Sant heard about Moore's own project, he was surprised. Though the two directors had met, and spent some time together years back during Moore's *The Big One* premiere in Nike headquarters' (and Van Sant's) hometown, Portland, Oregon, the director hadn't heard of *Bowling for Columbine* until production on his own film had started.

"We'd been working on our film [by then, but] we watched it before we made our film," Van Sant recalled. "I'm a big fan."

Released a year after *Bowling for Columbine*, Van Sant's *Elephant* would provide a completely different take on the tragedy. Using the camera as a mute witness, the main star of Van Sant's film was time itself. In the slow boredom of high school and suburbia, and the fractured time frame of the last day of life for several high school students unfolded, Van Sant further explained the differences between his and Moore's film: "I'm sure that Michael Moore made [*Bowling for Columbine*] for the same reasons. I think that his film, unlike maybe *Elephant*, is searching for direct answers, like, 'Too many bullets,' 'Too many guns.' These specific things were what Michael was after. In our film," Van Sant clarified, "we were thinking of those things but we were never really . . .

trying to label it or spell it out. I guess because of the intensity of the event. It's too big to maybe just stamp it, like 'Alienation,' 'Guns,' 'Bullets.' It's too amorphous. We wanted our film to work around that, and have ideas floating around and have the viewers involved in that, as opposed to just telling the viewers what to think."

For Moore, no event would be too big to be included in his sometimes brilliant, sometimes unwieldy thesis. One element in Moore's film, not in Gus Van Sant's, was the notion of bowling. The Littleton Sheriff's Office reported that, the morning of the Columbine shootings, the two killers calmly went to their 6:15 bowling class. To Moore, as he stated throughout the film, bowling was as likely a "reason" for the massacre as the theories of the media pundits, who touted everything from the influence of shock-rocker Marilyn Manson's songs to the violent video games played by the young men. Yet, on another level, by invoking bowling in the movie's title and as his centerpiece gag, Moore was drawing attention to America's cavalier attitude toward firearms. Shooting is a weekend pastime, and a constitutionally guaranteed one according to the Michigan militia who open the film. Nowhere is this attitude more frightening than in the interview Moore conducted with James Nichols — organic farmer from Michigan, brother to Oklahoma bomber Terry Nichols, and friend of Timothy McVeigh. In *Bowling for Columbine*, Nichols appeared tense and, by the end of the interview, possibly dangerous. Even Moore himself was concerned, as he tried to diffuse the moment when Nichols put a loaded gun to his own temple.

The filming of the interview lasted five hours. "He just went on and on," Moore said. "He was brilliant in the description of his beliefs, I had to hone that thing down to what you see in the film." Eventually, Nichols would initiate a defamation of character lawsuit against Moore for the way he appeared onscreen.

While making *Bowling for Columbine*, Moore was also writing his next book, *Stupid White Men*, an assault on what he saw as a sham election worthy of sanctions from the United Nations: the 2000 presidential win by George W. Bush. If Moore had trouble keeping his unique film together, Bush also struggled in that first year to find a tone for his presidency amid continued jokes and suspicions about his win. The destinies of both men would change on September 11, 2001, when four planes were hijacked by Al Qaeda operatives, two of which crashed into, and reduced to molten rubble, the World Trade Center, eliminating 2750 lives inside it. For some, the actions of the president following the attack, including the invasions of Afghanistan and Iraq, would be seen as brinkmanship. Instead of a backlash against the vague "evil-doers" and a quickly drummed-up retaliation bombing campaign, what could the president's reaction have been to September 11? For much of the rest of the world, including the millions globally who marched against the invasion of Iraq (in the largest single-issue protest ever) these actions could be summed up by the words of activist actor Alec Baldwin, who said, "We blew it, we could have united the world, but instead we pushed it away." Bush's actions would shape the rest of Moore's work on *Bowling for Columbine*, as Moore watched a world-stage demonstration of America's self-feeding loop of irrational fear.

This would be Moore's boldest move yet. Before

September 11, Bush had been considered a lame-duck president, headed for a single term footnote and tainted by the biggest electoral investigation in decades. After September 11, the oval office became immune to any criticism from the media. To criticize the President was to criticize all of America. As *Bowling for Columbine* neared completion, U.S. officials seemed to fulfill the film's prophesies, hastily passing "Patriot Acts," and perpetuating myths of letter bombs and anthrax attacks.

Even before the film made it to theaters, Moore faced down the publisher of his book — only after September 11. Written in Moore's patented clunky-but-spunky style during the Bush administration's first year, *Stupid White Men* described the election as a "coup" and documented George W. Bush's corporate history and shady moments. According to Moore, after September 11, HarperCollins wanted to pulp the copies of *Stupid White Men* already in print, and requested that he drastically rewrite the material so the President would appear in a better light. Lisa Herling, director of corporate communications for HarperCollins, stated, "as with any political book, you want to make sure it hasn't become outdated or need any adjustment based on the events of 9/11." Moore refused this highly irregular request to rewrite post-printing — and it was agreed that the book would be killed.

However, on December 1, 2001, a New Jersey librarian named Ann Sparanese heard Moore's story as he addressed the annual New Jersey Citizens Action conference. Within days, librarian chat rooms and Web sites were fierce with activity: the publisher became deluged with E-mails from angry librarians. By the end of December, HarperCollins agreed to release the book, without changes, in February. The book hit No. 1 in Canada and England, as well as on the *New York Times* bestseller list, remaining on the list for thirty-four weeks, even though the paper did not review the book. According to Moore, 90% of newspapers ignored the book.

Yet Moore found himself (along with another sudden bestselling author, Noam Chomsky) reaching his strangest audience yet as a voice of dissent in the post 9/11 world: mainstream America. As Moore embarked on his second forty-seven-city tour (booked not by Harper-Collins but by his two sisters, Anne and Veronica), he told the *Village Voice*, "I look out at the auditorium or gymnasium, and I don't see the tree huggers and the granola heads. . . . I see Mr. and Mrs. Middle America who voted for George W. Bush, who just lost $60,000 because their 401(k) is gone. And they believed in the American Dream as it was designed by the Bushes and Wall Street, and then they woke up to realize it was just that, a dream."

Within weeks, more than 500,000 copies of *Stupid White Men* were in print; within months Moore was again a figure of national interest, now considered a serious influence on the political landscape. In May 2002, Moore switched publishers, going over to Warner Books for a $3 million deal for his next two titles. And soon, *Bowling for Columbine* would eclipse even the success of *Stupid White Men*.

In May, buzz for the film had already started: *Bowling for Columbine* was welcomed into the Cannes Film Festival, who bent their own rules, allowing a documentary into competition for the first time in more than fifty years. Even with his wife and daughter at his side, Moore was overwhelmed — even more so when the film received a nearly fifteen-minute standing ovation. David Lynch presented Moore's film with the 55th Anniversary Prize at Cannes, and Moore's name was in every French newspaper. But just as Moore was at the top of his game, operating on volume 11, something happened to deeply undercut the pleasure of personal success, reminding him of a world beyond politics, interviews, or accolades — his mother died. The momentum he had been carefully building for years came to an abrupt stop. Canceling speaking dates that were pre-publicity for the film's American release, Michael went home. At the age of fifty-two, he was once again just a boy from Davison, spending a good portion of his summer simply being with his father.

On August 5, 2002, attempting to explain this portion of his life to his fan base, Michael wrote simply and from the heart:

> Dear friends,
> Four weeks ago today, my mother died. Her name was Veronica Moore. Someday I will write about who she was and what she meant to me in my life and the lives of everyone she touched. But I cannot do that today. The grief I have experienced in this past month has only barely subsided. Her passing was sudden and unexpected, though she got to live eighty-one wonderful years. I owe her everything. I am who I am because of her and my dad, and none of what I do or have done has been possible without the love and support they have given me.

Michael nearly didn't attend his own premiere at the Toronto Film Festival that September, but in the end, he did, driving from Flint with his father. Michael wasn't the type to allow grief to stop him from finishing what he had started. After a glowing response in Toronto, he eventually returned to New York, and the life of a busy award-winning film director. The film played festivals — and received honors — everywhere from Kansas to Amsterdam; from Sao Paulo, Brazil, to Montreal; from Bergen, Norway, to Tehran. Released in theaters that October, running two hours in length, the American buzz for *Bowling for Columbine* started slowly. The picture appeared first at select theaters on October 18, then juggernauted across North America to become the most successful non-music documentary ever. Earning over $60 million theatrically, its reception was bolstered partly by the still bestselling *Stupid White Men*, but also by the U.S.-led Iraq invasion that had, in the intervening months, divided the country more sharply than anything post-Vietnam.

While critics of Moore's politics debated his facts, creating innumerable Web sites that disparaged his name, film critics responded favorably, though they did point out that his weaknesses — self-aggrandisement and smugness — were still his weaknesses. Moore, however, heard the word "Oscar" being whispered for the first time since *Roger & Me*. In January 2003, it was announced that *Bowling for Columbine* had been nominated for Best Documentary. With no television show to deal with, and promotion winding down for both his book and film, Moore stopped moving for the first time in two years, retreating to his Michigan home before the March Academy Award ceremony. The rest would be needed, as it would be his last for some time. He geared up again for

Wednesday, February 26, 2003 — his return trip to Littleton. At 8 p.m., at the University of Denver, Moore entered the Magness Arena, an 8000-person packed theater — to the sound of cheers. It was more than he could have hoped for.

Just five days before the Academy Awards, in spite of a divided home country and worldwide condemnation (save for England), the U.S. invaded Iraq. The media became lively with guesses about what Moore would say should he receive the statue. When he did, in fact, take the prize, Moore would explain, "the history has been that the popular documentaries don't win . . . so frankly, I didn't think we had a chance of winning, and frankly I didn't come prepared with a speech." Near the time the documentary category's winner was to be announced, Moore was overcome with the panic of, "What if we did win?" Not knowing what to do, he leaned over to the other documentarians and asked that in the event that *Bowling* won, would they want to go up to the stage with him? He added the warning that he might say something about Bush. "They were wearing peace pins and they all said that they'd be honored."

Actor Diane Lane took the stage and read the nominees. Opening the envelope she sighed, smiled, and shouted, "*Bowling for Columbine*, Michael Moore!"

Moore, Glynn, and the other filmmakers took the stage as the audience rose to a standing ovation. Accepting the award, Moore said, "On behalf of our producers Kathleen Glynn, and Michael Donovan from Canada, I'd like to thank the Academy for this. I have invited my fellow documentary nominees on the stage with us, and we would like to — they're here in solidarity with me because we

EMILY SCHULTZ

like nonfiction. We like nonfiction and we live in fictitious times. We live in the time where we have fictitious election results that elect a fictitious president. We live in a time where we have a man sending us to war for fictitious reasons. Whether it's the fiction of duct tape or fiction of orange alerts, we are against this war, Mr. Bush. Shame on you, Mr. Bush, shame on you! And any time you got the Pope and the Dixie Chicks against you, your time is up. Thank you very much."

During the speech, in a clear display of the country's mood, half the audience stood and clapped; half booed. Moore later admitted that before he started, "there was a moment where I thought I could just soak up all the love and be off and have my great Oscar moment." Moore fought through to the end of his speech and went, as winners traditionally are sent, to the pressroom. Perhaps still nervous, and inadvertently revealing the dictatorial side his coworkers have hinted at over the years, Moore barked at the press, "Don't say there was a split decision in the hall because five loud people booed. Do your job and tell the truth."

Later, in a short documentary about the evening appearing on the *Bowling for Columbine* DVD, Moore admitted to hearing a mix of clapping and booing, a cacophony that was, to him, the sound of democracy. "Was it appropriate?" he asked. "I had made a film about violence and we were in the fifth day of a war I felt unjust and wrong . . . it fit perfectly with why I made this film." He concluded with a nod to his persona. "At the end of the day . . . I'm Michael Moore. What else was I going to do?"

Regardless of audience reaction, standing at the podium of the 2003 Academy Awards, accepting honors for the most profitable documentary film in history, Moore had bested Pauline Kael — and reached the enviable position of being able to pick and choose projects. He had left the movie assembly line of pinching and scraping for parts and funds.

As a postscript, it should be noted that one important bowling shot did not make it into Moore's film. Just after Moore's Oscar win, in May 2003, the Littleton Sheriff's Office released to the public a videotape they had confiscated in the wake of the shootings at Columbine. The video was of Eric Harris and Dylan Klebold target-practicing weeks before their rampage. Their targets? Bowling pins.

CHAPTER NINE

Moore Smokes 'Em Out

Fahrenheit 9/11

> Let me tell you something: *no* filmmaker wants to go through this kind of controversy. It does *not* sell tickets . . . I made this movie so people could see it as soon as possible. This is a huge and unwanted distraction.
>
> — *Michael Moore on being dropped by the Walt Disney Company*

In the business world in early 2004, one story dominated, and Michael Moore was in the middle of it. He took pains to explain that he just wanted to concentrate on film-making, but the wake from the scandal that involved him,

Miramax films, and the Disney corporation, would push *Fahrenheit 9/11* to the highest shores of success.

The relationship between the Disney corporation and one-time indie maverick Miramax films was long considered a relationship of strange bedfellows: the two companies couldn't be more different. Starting in the late '80s producing B-fare like slasher-pic *The Burning*, and mafia comedy *The Pope Must Die*, Miramax was founded by the Weinstein brothers, Harvey and Bob. Cutthroat business skills equally matched by a love of cinema resulted in the company's meteoric rise in the early '90s. With youth market hits *True Romance* and *Pulp Fiction* under their belts, the independent Miramax became an enticing buy for any large company, but heads shook in disbelief when that company turned out to be Disney. At the time, under the leadership of Michael Eisner, Disney was reveling in unprecedented profit margins after returning to the cutting edge of animation with *The Lion King* and *Toy Story*. With Disney funding and distribution, Miramax swept several Academy Awards (and made millions) with their art-house-for-the-suburbs style, but came to blows over more controversial films, such as Larry Clark's 1995 film, *Kids*.

By 2004, success had made a failure of the Disney/Miramax marriage. Disney was losing money after several financial disasters, including their ill-fated attempts to break into cable and Internet markets. Meanwhile, as producers of the *Lord of the Rings* trilogy, the Weinsteins had become the most powerful team in Hollywood. With corporate divorce imminent, Moore, in a stroke of good timing, found himself in the midst of a lovers' quarrel, and walked away with a film budgeted at $6 million.

Echoing his other battles, this one was another He Said/ He Said situation, but instead of being the hot topic at potlucks, it was the hot topic of power lunches everywhere, and soon enough, was national news.

It was one month after his Oscar win that Moore announced his next project was going to be an exposé of the links between the Bush and Bin Laden families. Recalling the 1976 film, *Network*, Moore intended to investigate a collusion of corporate America, the media, and arms manufacturers. At the age where many begin to think of taking early retirement, Moore and Glynn told *U.S.A Today* that they'd considered quitting film after *Bowling for Columbine*, but the comment now seems more like false modesty, as Moore was setting aside his film project *Sicko* — a film about the American health care system (now projected for 2006) — to pursue George W. Bush with a visual impact his 2003 book, *Dude, Where's My Country?*, could not provide.

The belief that corporations, and not the people, pick elected leaders through a nexus of fundraising and lobbying is now entrenched, almost a core American value shared by everyone from President Dwight D. Eisenhower (whose final 1961 speech, warning of useless involvement in Vietnam, coined the phrase "military industrial complex") to domestic terrorist Timothy McVeigh. On one hand, rigorous analysis by economists and philosophers does indicate that the stock market determines policy more than the will of the people. However, many, including activist theorist Noam Chomsky, stress that there is no "conspiracy" to it. There is no star chamber of men in suits (as presented in the pop paranoia of TV's *The X-Files*), just a system that allows it to happen — the tendency of the rich to socialize with the rich, and strive to make life better for themselves. The subtleties of Chomsky's "systems analysis" were not ready-made for the large audience that *Bowling for Columbine*'s success would guarantee, but the promise of illicit information and shadowy connections played into the grand drama of an American consciousness distrustful of its elected officials since Watergate, and inflamed by the still-hot topic of the 2000 election results. *Fahrenheit 9/11* ended up being completely different from Moore's original vision, and what was different about it was what audiences, from Cannes to Kansas, responded to.

But even before there was a film, there was the issue of funding and distribution that threatened to overshadow the picture itself. When Moore had announced *Fahrenheit 9/11* in April 2003, he also announced that Miramax had agreed to fund and distribute the picture, with filming to begin that May, and a firm release date of July 2004. That a documentary could be released in a month reserved for blockbusters — as well as funded by a subsidiary of Disney — was proof of the success Moore had achieved.

Filming began, and was uneventful except for the fact that Moore was choosing not to include himself in the picture. As he told reporters, "It was a conscious decision . . . The material was so strong that a little bit of me goes a long way." This decision, however, caused him to have numerous battles with Harvey Weinstein, who insisted that it was Moore whom audiences would be paying to see. As Moore had stated earlier, he'd only appeared in *Roger & Me* out of technical ineptitude on his part (not knowing where to stand), then turned that ineptitude into technique, feeling his subjects were more comfortable on camera when he was standing beside them. "If you look like me," Moore once joked with the *Stanford Daily*, "would you have this incredible ego where you'd want to see yourself blown-up forty-feet on a movie screen? 'Oh, put me in another shot, I look so good there, ah!' . . . I can't stand it. That's a horrible, horrible feeling. You'd have to live your life in my body to understand this."

Moore appears fleetingly in the finished *Fahrenheit 9/11*, which has a three-part structure given over to Bush's contested connections to Bin Laden, the implications of the Patriot Act, and the Iraq War (declared "over" long before thousands of American soldiers were killed) as told through the voice of one Flint mother who lost her son. To illustrate that most of Congress had not read the Patriot Act before passing it, Moore took to the streets of Washington, D.C., with a truck and a loudspeaker, reading the act for the benefit of everyone on Capitol Hill. Compared to the rest of the film, this sequence feels like a holdover from the days of freewheeling cynicism on *The Awful Truth*.

In February 2004, production on *Fahrenheit 9/11* was close to finished when the news hit that the Weinstein brothers would be stepping down from their posts at the company they'd founded and named after their parents, Mira and Max. There were whispers of buyout packages of $100 million. In the background of this erupting news — but soon to be pushed to the foreground — was Moore's film and its contested history. It would explode across headlines just as *Fahrenheit 9/11* was being delivered for competition at the Cannes Film Festival.

In the public's mind, the Cannes Film Festival exudes

a sense of respect and artistic integrity. It is, however, very much a trade show, where thousands of movies are sold and deals are made on the run by people selling Hungarian rights for teen market movies like *Halloween: Resurrection* on one cell phone and cable rights for art-house hits like *The Sweet Hereafter* on the other. *Fahrenheit 9/11* arrived with a pedigree of controversy. Only a week earlier, after rumors of trouble in Disney/ Miramax paradise began hitting the papers, Moore received the official phone call. Though Miramax had tried to persuade Disney, they had to break the news that they could not distribute the film. It was then that competing stories about what had been promised began to circulate. With the Weinstein brothers negotiating their way out of the company, the last word was fought over by the two Mikes — Eisner and Moore. Moore stated that only a month after signing the distribution deal, Eisner requested a meeting with his agent, Ari Emanuel, to express his extreme displeasure over the *Fahrenheit* project. Moore claimed Eisner's biggest concern was angering Florida Governor Jeb Bush, brother to the president and an important player in much of Disney's theme-park businesses and licences.

"Eisner did not call Miramax and tell them to stop my film," Moore said later. "Not only that, for the next year, SIX MILLION dollars of DISNEY money continued to flow into the production of making my movie. Miramax assured me that there were no distribution problems with my film."

After Eisner's meeting with Moore's agent, nothing more was heard until *Fahrenheit 9/11* was selected for competition at Cannes, and Disney sent an executive to New York to watch a preview screening. It was this screening that led to Disney dropping the film. Eisner countered that Moore had known for that past year Miramax would not distribute the film. That money was given to the production after Eisner's meeting with Moore's agent came as a complete shock to Eisner and Disney. Eisner continued to claim Harvey Weinstein had hidden the $6 million to *Fahrenheit* as a "bridge loan" in paperwork for other productions. Weinstein could have settled this debate, but he was mired in his own negotiations against Disney, so kept silent, except to say that, with Moore, he would buy the film back contingent on a worldwide distributor. Given the timing of the film in Miramax's corporate relationship with Disney, and what ultimately happened, it is possible that Weinstein had calculated all this in advance, wanting to antagonize Disney by using *their* money to make a film he knew they would not distribute, then taking it off their hands cheap. Any publicity gained from this approach couldn't hurt either. Without a distributor, amidst corporate intrigue and rumors regarding the actual content of the film, *Fahrenheit 9/11* entered the Cannes Film Festival, and on May 22nd, 2004, became the second documentary ever to win the coveted Palme D'Or prize.

Phrases like "twenty-minute standing ovation" and "politically motivated" began appearing on op-ed and Internet pages across the world, though much of the world had not yet seen the film. The *Village Voice* commented that the jury of the 57th festival was "wearing its politics on its sleeve." Jury president Quentin Tarantino responded that it was bravura filmmaking — and not politics — that had motivated the jury's decision. Some might humorously suggest a Detroit conspiracy (Tarantino spent his twenties there), but upon closer examination of the film, his assessment might prove correct.

After winning the award, Moore had cockily declared his film would have a distributor inside twenty-four hours. However, his usual strict demands interfered with interest. The release date of July 2004 had to be guaranteed; a November release for the home video market had to be guaranteed; a "free rental day" at video stores in November had to be guaranteed. These dates, of course, were timed with the U.S. presidential primaries and election; they were Moore's way of turning what would be the year's most famous film into a tool for voter activism. In the end, some, but not all, of his demands would be met.

While at Cannes, Moore spoke to another political filmmaker, George Gittoes, one of Australia's most respected artists. Gittoes expressed his surprise to see footage from his own film as the centerpiece for *Fahrenheit 9/11*. Like Moore, Gittoes' approach has put him in a gray area between activism and art; he travels the globe to strife-ridden areas to find his subjects. During his visits to Iraq, Gittoes filmed the unique, powerful, and disturbing documentary, *Soundtrack To War*. Realizing that most soldiers in the U.S. Army were between the ages of eighteen and twenty-two, a time when music is important to identity, Gittoes asked soldiers about the music in their lives. He discovered that all Army vehicles and communications systems are wired for music as well. Gangsta hip-hop and metal play as soldiers psych themselves for battle, and as bombs drop. This much appears in Moore's *Fahrenheit 9/11*, but what was left out was the human element Gittoes was trying to show: militias playing music during downtime, freestyle rapping during the interminable boredom that occurs between the short bursts of absolute terror that is a soldier's life during war. "Music is more important to us than food here," one soldier told Gittoes.

Gittoes claimed "there are about seventeen scenes from my documentary in his film. I wouldn't go so far as to say he lifted [them]. Michael got access to my stuff and assumed that I would be happy for it to be in 9/11. I would actually have been quite happy for it not to be in 9/11." The Australian had sold the footage to a company called Westside Productions, and did not know it would be used for one of Moore's films. His interview with an Australian newspaper hinted at his annoyance at how his footage was presented, but in a backhanded compliment, said that he was glad people would see his footage even if he himself had "made a better movie." The interview ended with Gittoes' statement that he would let the treatment of his scenes slide. Illustrative of the tension surrounding Moore's film even early in its release, once these quotes reached the Internet, Moore was under bombardment: the story had mutated to Moore stealing scenes without paying Gittoes.

In a 2005 interview with Australian film magazine, *Filmink*, Gittoes revealed his reasons for keeping relatively quiet about the use of the clips in 9/11, "It's a problematic issue that I can't talk about because I've signed a legal deal with Michael not to talk about it . . . so many people wanted to crucify Michael Moore in the buildup to the election and I didn't want to give anyone ammunition. So I couldn't really release my film theatrically at the same time as his . . . I would have loved it to have had a theatrical life but it was eclipsed by *Fahrenheit 9/11*."

As promised by Moore, *Fahrenheit 9/11* does begin as a polemic against the administration of George W. Bush.

Footage of cabinet members being prepped for press conferences is eerie, foreboding. Before Bush is set to declare war on Iraq, he is, as Moore described it to the *New York Times*, joking like a schoolboy. As cinema, this first portion of the film fails. Summing up decades of international finance and policy in less than forty minutes' screen time was necessary to Moore's thesis, but also displayed his weaknesses as a filmmaker. Moore works best as a polemicist, not a journalist. What continues to irk his critics is that while he never claims to be a journalist directly, he does so indirectly, by stating, as he often has, that if journalists were doing their jobs, he wouldn't have to do his. And what would that make *his* job?

The links between the Bush empire and the strange world of international oil has been debated and explored for the last several years in journalism both honed and sloppy. And so the "facts" in this section of Moore's film were hotly debated, threatening to overshadow what audiences, and not pundits, actually responded to. What followed the first section of the film has not been debated; it was something entirely different.

Moore's strength as a filmmaker is his ability to explore and display the effect of international policy and finance on the everyday world. *Fahrenheit 9/11* heated up only when it left Bush as a subject, since the President appeared in the film as more of an abstraction than a person. When the film shifts to the reality of Iraq — of smoke, blood, and destroyed flesh — it leaves partisan politics behind and becomes a simple plea for some shred of respect for human life. From here, the film returns to the United States to follow two recruitment officers whose jobs included brazenly searching for soldiers in poor, non-white regions.

EMILY SCHULTZ

Rundown malls were depicted as their bread and butter, and the recruitment officers appeared equally like vampires and bumbling detectives. If the emotional center of *Roger & Me* was the Bunny Lady, then *Fahrenheit 9/11*'s emotional center was another Flint woman. Lila Lipscomb is a patriotic American who, in the time it took to make the film, lost her son to fighting in Iraq. Her travels to Washington, D.C., to find answers brought her into contact with a mourning Iraqi woman. That meeting became one of the most emotionally charged in the film and, strangely, the least manipulative. A mother's tears and questions cannot by explained away by sound bites, left or right politics, nor can the answers live up to the senseless pain and loss of a parent who has had to bury her child. As the *New York Times* commented upon the film's U.S. release, "Mr. Bush is under no obligation to answer Mr. Moore's charges, but he will have to answer to Mrs. Lipscomb."

With Moore's Bush "revelations" debated unto numbness by pundits, the power of the film, and what brought people into the theaters in record numbers, lay in its denouement, which, in only two or three scenes, put its finger on the pulse of an angry and confused American public. By the time the film found distribution and released in the U.S., the *Village Voice* would change its tune from its earlier Palme D'Or rejoinder, reviewing Moore's work more favorably: "The film may not earn points for subtlety, but on the other hand it persuasively damns current government mendacity with a final, heart-wrenching segment. Besides, subtlety in American politics stands as much chance of being noticed as a sleeping man in a room full of the newly dead. Moore will be Moore, and we won't be the less for it."

The *New York Times*, though still candidly pointing out the film's failures, would encourage viewers of all political persuasions to the theaters: "It may be that the confusions trailing Mr. Moore's narrative are what make *Fahrenheit 9/11* an authentic and indispensable document of its time. The film can be seen as an effort to wrest clarity from shock, anger, and dismay, and if parts of it seem rash, overstated or muddled, well, so has the national mood." *Times* writer A.O. Scott continued, "if *Fahrenheit 9/11* consisted solely of talking heads and unflattering glimpses of public figures, it would be, depending on your politics, either a rousing call to arms or an irresponsible provocation, but it might not persuade you to reexamine your assumptions." Scott went on to recommend it to all, regardless of political persuasion.

Even Moore's nemesis during the early days of *Roger & Me*, former *Film Comment* magazine editor Harlan Jacobson, conceded in *U.S.A Today* that *Fahrenheit 9/11* was powerful, though he couldn't resist adding a barb against Moore's ambitious personality, saying, "it's one thing to have a strong political view, it's another to savage people using questionable tactics, and making fun of people while portraying yourself as a man of the proletariat." Moore would face the same criticisms he had always faced, but as they say in the media business, no press is bad press; even condemnations meant Moore's name was being dropped into the ears of a nation.

Several tense weeks after Cannes and the Disney debacle, Moore could breathe a sigh of relief. It was announced that worldwide distribution of *Fahrenheit 9/11* would be handled by Lions Gate Films, a Canadian company that had previously taken Kevin Smith's hot-potato dud, *Dogma*, off Miramax's hands. In the U.S., the Independent Film Channel would handle theatrical distribution. On the heels of the front-page treatment of its distribution woes, its Cannes' win, and as fighting raged in the streets of Iraq, *Fahrenheit 9/11* opened, as planned, on June 23. In its opening weekend, it grossed $24 million, and was the No. 1 movie in North America.

If one wanted to measure the distance Moore had traveled in thirteen years, one need look no further than the differences between the premieres of *Fahrenheit 9/11* and Moore's first film, *Roger & Me*. The premiere of the new film was attended by glittering celebrities of the Hollywood left, and a few rock stars for good measure. Written up in the *Times* Style section, *Fahrenheit 9/11* had actor Leonardo DiCaprio in attendance. Showing both in New York City and Washington, D.C. (the official world premiere), there were swaths of red carpet, and half of the Democratic left in attendance, many on Moore's personal guest list. Thirteen years earlier, the New York *Roger & Me* premiere included a kitschy party with beans and franks, the premise of which offended Glynn, while the "Invitational World Premiere" was at a multiplex outside Flint, with Rivethead Ben Hamper in attendance. Yet at both of these worlds-apart premieres, Moore could be seen in a baseball cap and his jeans. What had changed could be summed up in the words of the *Times* columnist Joyce Wadler: "We had, we must admit, some concerns about Mr. Moore. The normally approachable fellow, wearing his usual schlumpy jacket and green Michigan State University baseball cap, had been guarded by a ferocious little press agent whom he permitted to rebuff reporters as he rushed into the screening."

As its release snowballed, *Fahrenheit 9/11* became not a movie but a phenomenon, selling out theaters for days, and ultimately running on 2000 screens in North America, while grossing $222 million worldwide. Only two chains refused to screen the film. With theaters in Nebraska, Iowa, and the political rallying ground of Illinois, the restricted screens they owned were little match for the other 2000 screens showing the summer's hottest film. Like all phenomenon films, it became almost immune to critical reaction, in much the same way that *Star Wars* was never critiqued for its weak acting. The nation and the pundits were, however, waiting for the one critic that mattered to speak out on the issue, the White House. Moore was ready for anything. Following on *Bowling for Columbine*'s success, he could now afford to keep the kind of staff required to take on the President of the United States, who was ironically a first cousin of *Blood in the Face* director Kevin Rafferty, the first to help Moore launch his film career. In addition to a team of fact checkers during the film's editing, Moore had prepped a kind of "war room" to deal quickly with assaults on the film's credibility by conservative groups. Moore's team included Chris Lehane, a strategist of the Democratic Party, as well as fact-checking team formerly of the *New Yorker*, and a consulting squad of defamation suit lawyers. Without a shred of his usual humor, Moore declared, "We want the word out. Any attempts to libel me will be met by force."

Moore had wanted his film to be a lightning rod for dissatisfied voters who would, if not turn out for the polls, at least realize their own roles in the political process. Opinion from the executive office was a simple "outrageously false," courtesy of Presidential Communications Director Dan Bartlett, though reporters did manage to get the answer, "What do you think?" from First Lady Laura Bush, when asked if she had seen the film. That position changed as Bush's second run for the office became seriously threatened by Democratic challenger John Kerry. Polls consistently showed both a severe disapproval of Bush's handling of Iraq, and a marginal 2% lead over Kerry. As the Bush campaign realized that it would actually have to work for reelection, Moore's movie became not just a thorn in its side, but a serious threat that had to be dealt with. Various Republican groups across the country wanted screenings of the film stopped because, as David Bossie of Citizen's United said, "Moore has publicly indicated his goal is to impact this election," and this, he claimed, violated federal election laws. Ultimately, the White House was smart enough to not use federal powers to challenge a movie.

Instead, news networks appeared to be doing the dirty work. While the public waited for comments from Fox, featured none-too-favorably in the film, to put it mildly, the network remained tight-lipped. Their biggest complaint was that Moore had not granted them an interview. It was ABC and NBC who went on the offensive over the film, using the standard Michael Moore disparagement. ABC ran "Fact or Fiction?" captions across their screens during *Good Morning America* and *World News Tonight*, and NBC's *Nightly News* termed its coverage a "truth-squad report." While Moore responded to questions and criticisms of George Stephanopoulos on ABC's *This Week*, these responses were not used on *Good Morning America*, though it did run footage of Richard Clarke, the former security adviser who Moore insisted authorized the flights of Bin Ladens from America following the September 11 attacks. The publicist from *Good Morning America* later claimed Moore had been given a fair chance to respond to the criticisms leveled at his film. But Moore wasn't the only man who didn't think so.

"Note that none of the facts in *Fahrenheit 9/11* are in dispute," wrote Richard Goldstein in the *Village Voice*. "What ABC and NBC called into question is Moore's extrapolation and interpretation of information; in other words, his slant. But by using loaded phrases like 'truth squad' and 'fact or fiction,' and by omitting Moore's answers to key questions, these networks did the very thing they accuse him of doing. I would argue that this sort of distortion is far more dangerous in the context of a news broadcast than in a clearly opinionated film." Goldstein posited that NBC and ABC had good reason to disable Moore's film — that NBC was owned by General Electric, a major defense contractor, and ABC owned by Disney, a company largely affected by the laws of Florida where Bush's brother Jeb set state controls.

Goldstein also commented that considering how well the movie was doing in spite of the media bullying, one had to conclude that, in the end, the American public were still set on making up their own minds. In contrast, CNN and CBS took neutral positions, summarizing the ups and downs of the film that had everyone's temperatures rising. As Goldstein concluded in the *Village Voice*, "If the film turns out to have an impact on the fall election, we'll learn something about the limits of the media's power to shape perceptions . . . . I hope *Fahrenheit 9/11* affirms my conviction that the press distorts but we decide."

EMILY SCHULTZ

One thing everyone did agree on was the double-edged sword that *Fahrenheit 9/11* was for the Democratic Party. Until late in the election year, Moore was not a registered Democrat, and in fact, had been a vocal supporter of Ralph Nader during the 2000 election (their relationship eventually souring again). As far back as 1999, Moore accused John Kerry of being "a billionaire who wants to buy the presidency." The Kerry camp was ambivalent and silent. A senior advisor for the Kerry campaign stated that they shouldn't even acknowledge the film's existence lest they "get stuck with all that Michael Moore baggage."

If Moore had wanted *Fahrenheit* to be a partisan film whose sole goal was a Democrat victory, then both he and the Demo-cratic Party took a rather strange approach. Moore's real goal, however, was to engage the public in a political process they had long felt alienated from, and whose failure they had begun to accept with the regularity of Friday night television. It was Moore's questionable genius that he used the same techniques used to create Friday night television to great and frightening effect in *Fahrenheit 9/11*, the possible result being that the 2004 election had the largest voter turnout since 1968.

Some might point out that 1968 was the most intense year of the Vietnam War, and people are, naturally, more politicized at such times. However, if we are to believe the U.S. administration that there was no Iraq War, then the assumption left to us would be that it was Moore's "outrageously false" film that inflamed the polls. That's a bungle worthy of George W. Bush.

Conclusion

Citizen Moore

As F. Scott Fitzgerald once observed, "There are no second acts in American lives." Fitzgerald's observation was astute in regard to his own short career, yet if it were true of all American lives, then writing biographies of living subjects would not be so difficult. Michael Moore had already enjoyed several acts — journalist, writer, and filmmaker — yet in the year following the release of *Fahrenheit 9/11*, he was to walk onto the strangest stage yet: mainstream politics.

Orson Welles' *Citizen Kane* — to return to a fictional story of a journalist turned populist — has been interpreted as the tale of the first media tycoon, William Randolph Hearst, and the prefix "Citizen" is often pulled out to describe the Ted Turners and Conrad Blacks of the world. But in retrospect, Welles' story seems more a film about ideals — fought for, and lost. In the film, protagonist Charles Foster Kane starts his newspaper empire based on the unique premise that "the people" want the truth. To the consternation of those around him, including his own robber-baron associates, he tells "the people" the truth. Yet, to deliver the truth, Kane employs a loose populism, scare headlines that smooth over the frayed edges that streak any complex story. After this approach proves successful, Kane grows in power, and soon sees himself as the sole arbiter of truth, a hero of the people, ready for politics.

Citizen Kane might also be the first exploration of the blurring line between journalism and entertainment — a blurred line Moore has walked since the age of eighteen. That line is the source of all his strengths and, for his critics, of all his faults. In democratic societies, journalists are accorded, at least in theory, the same sacred status as Catholic Priests and psychiatrists — their sources are protected and they cannot be attacked by the state. Entertainers, on the other hand, are always bound by the limits of society and culture. Entertainers can push just enough, as in the political skits of *Saturday Night Live*, and be rewarded. They can also push too far for their times, like Lenny Bruce, and be crushed for it. As his career began its ascent in the late '90s, Moore used, to the consternation of even his associates on the left, the populist forms of entertainment to achieve the goals of journalism.

One of the immediate aftereffects of the successes of *Bowling for Columbine* and *Fahrenheit 9/11* was an upsurge in the popularity of political documentaries. *Control Room*, by Jehane Noujaim, was a searing, inside look at Al Jazeera, the other news channel. Errol Morris's *The Fog of War* was an exploration of the vagaries and meaning of Vietnam, and took home the Best Documentary Oscar a year after Moore's win. But making another film that could ride his own coattails was the farthest thing from Moore's mind as he entered his *Citizen Kane* year. Immediately after *Fahrenheit*'s release, Moore published *The Official Fahrenheit 9/11 Reader*, a collection including the script, articles on the movie, and most important, citations and support material for the claims made in his film regarding George W. Bush. The book amounted to a 363-page letter to the film's voluminous critics, both in the major media, and on crackpot Web sites that spent an inordinate amount of time criticizing the semiotic nuances of the film.

Another part of Moore's response was to concentrate his energies on "making sure as many people see this film as possible." So he launched his "Slacker Uprising" tour. Moore traveled the Big One yet again, this time in an attempt to motivate the age group that was generally the most listless in American electoral politics — youths in the 18–24 bracket. The term "slacker" had not been in vogue for more than a decade, and probably seemed quaint to the people who were four years old when Richard Linklater's film of the same name released in 1991. The Slacker tour collided with an already politically charged America. With everything that happened in the world after 9/11, the American public was invigorated in ways the country had not seen in years, guaranteeing a record turnout on Tuesday, November 2, 2004.

While touring, Moore also published the book, *Will They Ever Trust Us Again? Letters From the War Zone*. The title came from his final words in the *Fahrenheit 9/11* film narration, and refers to the poor citizens of the United States, who disproportionately make up the armed forces. A collection of letters of support and debate from soldiers stationed in Iraq, to even Moore's most ardent supporters, the book seemed like he was scraping from the bottom of the idea barrel. To his critics, the cover photo of Moore holding a small folded, funereal American flag in his giant hands (evoking either an All-State advertisement or a Jehovah's Witness pamphlet) was the last straw in a year that had already sent them into apoplexy. After a brief week of promising sales, the book disappeared off top-ten lists.

And Bush won the election. But he won with the narrowest margin for a sitting president since Woodrow Wilson's win in 1916. As many commentators pointed out, Bush's win was not the result of a soaring approval rating (with bodies arriving weekly from Iraq during the election campaign, his ratings were in fact, plummeting), but because the challenger proved less interesting. After brief flourishes, John Kerry left the impression that he was not the "next Kennedy," but a career politician, the kind of former-idealist-for-hire that accounts for most of the population of Capitol Hill. In Moore's own voter campaign during the election, his support of the Democratic Party — or lack of it — was an issue both he and Kerry danced around. Moore was spending months on the road, doing everything possible to make sure Bush would not be reelected, yet at the same time, he was not recommending any exact "who" as an alternative. In the (realistically speaking) two-party electoral system of America, this was a strange lacuna for the public to understand. It wasn't until the last moment that Moore threw his weight behind Kerry, begging his own fans to "spend these last twenty-four hours trying to convince whomever you can to show up and vote for John Kerry," urging Republicans to "give the new guy a chance," and saying to his friends on the left, "okay, Kerry isn't everything you wished he would be. You're right. He's not you! Or me. But we're not on the ballot — Kerry is."

In the *New York Times*, after the election, *The Fog of War* director Errol Morris said, "behind the liberal agenda — behind any agenda — is the idea 'I'm right, you're wrong.' My fear was that much of the material emerging from the left or from the Democrats was preaching to the choir. I sometimes look at *Fahrenheit 9/11* as creating a kind of secular church. You could go to the movie theater and collectively worship against the Bush infidel." In the year 2004, liberals produced better documentaries than candidates. In crude cinematic terms, George W. Bush played the method-acting heavy in dozens of documentaries, while the "hero" phoned-in his performance, Kerry's face seldom gracing the screen. If the numbers in attendance for Moore's Slacker Uprising speeches — and at the box office — were any indication, Moore might have stood a better chance against the president than the Democratic challenger.

Moore could not bring himself to throw his full support into the two-party system he had opposed all his life, and election night brought a strange end to his year as a significant opinion-maker. Readers may recall that that Moore had hinted at early retirement after *Bowling for Columbine*. It was an emotional period for Moore, of great critical and financial success on the one hand, and on the other, the grief of just losing his mother. But the successes of *Fahrenheit 9/11* drove Moore on to attempt change — not through the abstract medium of the screen, as he had since *Roger & Me*, but on the grassroots level he'd used back in the days of the Flint school board, and at the house on Lapeer Road. This change of direction also revealed Moore's limitations, imposed by his own sense of radicalism (and to his critics on the left, his cynicism). Moore can rile, he can inspire, impress, evaluate, and entertain; but he himself could not believe in the effectiveness of the system. His last-minute support for Kerry seemed like a human and panicked response rather than a calculation.

Unusual things had been achieved, however, whether through Moore's dogged efforts or through a social climate that had been a beehive of anger and doubt since September 11, 2001: the youth in America turned out to the polls in record numbers. *The Boston Globe* reported that "despite long lines and registration snafus, voters under age thirty clocked the highest turnout percentage since 1972." Not only that, but on the afternoon of Thursday, January 6, 2005, to use Moore's words, "something historic happened. For the first time since 1877, a member of the House and a member of the Senate stood up together to object to a state's electoral college votes. . . . California Senator Barbara Boxer rose to the occasion, and stood with Ohio Representative Stephanie Tubbs Jones and thirty other Representatives 'to cast the light of truth on a flawed system which must be fixed now.'" Bush had won the election, but "Michael Moore" was still the name being bandied about on the floor of the senate. Representative Maxine Waters even went so far as to dedicate her objection to Ohio's electoral votes to "Mr.

Michael Moore, the producer of the documentary *Fahrenheit 9/11*," with her thanks for "educating the world on the threats to our democracy, and the proceedings of this house on the acceptance of the electoral college votes for the 2000 presidential election." That thin line Moore had walked between art and politics had just been crossed.

In the months following the election, Moore was silent for the first time in four years. He announced the start of production on *Fahrenheit 9/11 and a 1/2*, a sequel to be released in the election year of 2008. Will it have the same urgency as its predecessor? Probably not. With term limitations, Bush cannot run for president again, and as Bush's own father and Al Gore proved, vice presidents have a habit of not winning. With little hope for Dick Cheney, this leaves the rumors of Hillary Clinton as the Democratic challenger — a choice we know the infatuated Moore would wholeheartedly support.

Closer on the horizon is *Sicko*, Moore's documentary on the failure of the healthcare system in the United States, and the tendency of pharmaceutical giants to shape public policy for profit. The *Sicko* project began while Moore was still working on *Bowling for Columbine*, and has been pushed around his plate for almost three years. With an unprecedented number of Americans now of retirement age, and health care and Social Security becoming the hot domestic issue of Bush's second term, *Sicko* may not only signal a return to a tighter form for Moore, but increase his popularity as a filmmaker and cultural voice.

There has been one public appearance from Moore that has remained in many minds. To attend the 2005

People's Choice Awards — where *Fahrenheit 9/11* was nominated for Best Film, and won via a voting poll of 21 million — Moore received his first makeover. While the moment wasn't as striking as the one in pop history when rock band KISS removed their makeup, Moore's official restyling was noticed. In his acceptance speech, characteristically, Moore stressed that "the people" (the majority of 21 million of them, in fact) had voted for his film, yet he himself appeared less like the average Joe, and more like what he actually *is*: a successful filmmaker. Gone were the baseball cap, the relaxed-fit jeans, and windbreaker — replaced by a tailored designer suit. Moore's Michigan-mop of a hairstyle was shorn down to a hip, spiky cut, and his twelve-day beard trimmed into a goatee with its gray dyed out.

As Walt Whitman wrote in *Song of Myself,* "I contain multitudes." We will have to wait for Moore's next film to see if his awareness of who he was, and who he has become, can be contained in one personality; whether he can still be "just a guy from Michigan," as well as one of the most divisive and controversial filmmakers of our time. There is one thing we "the people" do not need to wait on, though, and that is the understanding that Michael Moore, as cultural provocateur and leader, has very much arrived.

EMILY SCHULTZ

Acknowledgements

The author wishes to give warm thanks to the interview subjects of this book for their thoughtfulness and openness, including: John Derevlany, Walter Gasparovic, Alan Edelstein, Ryan Eashoo, and Anonymous. Thanks also to the *Flint Journal*, the Flint Public Library, the University of Michigan Library, the Sloan Museum in Flint, and Queen Video in Toronto (Queen Street West).

Thank you to my editor, Kevin Connolly, my publisher, Jack David, associate editor Crissy Boylan, and everyone at ECW Press.

Sources

Introduction
Bonzo Goes to Bitburg

Kolmeshohe Cemetery story and quote: Michael Moore, *Michigan Voice*, Burton, Michigan, June/July 1985, pp. 6–10.

Moore's response to Pauline Kael: Michael Moore, "Pauline Kael, the Truth, and Nothing But ... Brought to you by AOL Time Warner," January 12, 2000, http://www.michaelmoore.com/words/message/index.php?messageDate=2000-01-12.

Chapter 1
Just a Guy from Michigan
Inside/Outside Flint

Description of Lodge Freeway as slabs of steel: Ben Schmitt, "Looking Back: Freeway marvel of 1955," *Detroit Free Press*, September 24, 2004, Friday 3 Edition.

Reference to Pat Boone as "Mr. Chevrolet Himself": Michael Moore, *Roger & Me*, 1989.

Depopulation of Flint, Michigan, documents from 1970 census to year 2000: U.S. Census Bureau, 2000, http://www.census.gov/srd/papers/pdf/ev92-24.pdf and http://censtats.census.gov/cgi-bin/pct/pctProfile.pl.

The settling of Flint: Microsoft Encarta Online Encyclopedia, 2001,
http://encarta.msn.com.

GM history and Alfred P. Sloane quote:
http://www.buyandhold.com/bh/en/education/history/2001/
generalmotors.html.

Grievances and Flint sit-down strike:
http://www.historicalvoices.org/flint/organization.php.

Quote from Flint woman whose husband intended to strike: audio
file of speaker, Rollin Moon. Interviewed by U-M Flint Labor
History Project. Date of interview: 05-10-1979. Edited by Michael
Van Dyke. Michigan State University, 2002,
http://www.historicalvoices.org/flint/organization.php.

Types of entertainment during Flint sit-down strike: audio file of
speaker, Earl Hubbard. Interviewed by U-M Flint Labor History
Project. Date of interview: 21-04-1980. Edited by Michael Van
Dyke. Michigan State University, 2002,
http://www.historicalvoices.org/flint/organization.php.

Story regarding burning burlap during Flint sit-down strike: audio
file of speaker, Earl Hubbard. Interviewed by U-M Flint Labor
History Project. Date of interview: 21-04-1980. Edited by
Michael Van Dyke. Michigan State University, 2002,
http://www.historicalvoices.org/flint/organization.php.

Rumor of being "shot out" during Flint sit-down strike: audio file of
speaker Mr. K. Gillian. Interviewed by U-M Flint Labor History
Project. Date of interview: 15-07-1978. Edited by Michael Van
Dyke. Michigan State University, 2002, http://www.histori-
calvoices.org/flint/organization.php.

Moore's regularity of attending movies: Michael Moore, commentary, *Roger & Me*, 2003, DVD.

Moore disliking school, "bored beyond belief," and ABC's song:
Michael Moore, *Stupid White Men*, ReganBooks, New York, 2004
paperback edition, pp. 97–99.

Moore and the "3C's": Michael Moore, "High School Graduation,"
June 11, 1999,
http://www.michaelmoore.com/words/message/index.php?mess
ageDate=1999-06-11.

Moore on long hair and drugs: Mark Binelli, "Michael Moore: 'To be
the object of so much venom from all the wrong people you

must be doing something right,'" *Rolling Stone*, New York, September 2004, Issue No. RS957, pp. 67–69.

Don Hammond on Michael Moore's behavior in meetings: Shawn Windsor, "Moore missing from hall of fame," *Detroit Free Press*, January 14, 2005, Friday 1 Edition.

Moore youngest elected person to school board: Michael Moore, "The Day I Was to Be Tarred and Feathered," December 12, 1999, http://www.michaelmoore.com/words/message/index.php?messageDate=1999-12-12.

Moore's actions while serving on school board and the ballot to remove him: *ibid.*

Ben Hamper on visiting his father at the Fisher 1 plant on "family night": Ben Hamper, *Rivethead: Tales From the Assembly Line.* Warner Books Inc., New York, 1986, p. 1. See also: http://www.michaelmoore.com/hamper/excerpt1.html

Moore's heroes who escaped the life in the factory: Michael Moore, *Roger & Me*, 1989.

Hamper on shoprats and ancestors with an automotive dream: Ben Hamper, *Rivethead: Tales From the Assembly Line*, Warner Books Inc., New York, 1986, p. 5. See also: http://www.michaelmoore.com/hamper/excerpt1.html

Moore quote on not going into the factory: Michael Moore, Scene 3, "Back to Flint," Commentary, *Roger & Me*, 2003, DVD.

Chapter Two
Born to Run and the Spirit of '76

Moore drops out of University of Michigan over lack of parking space: *Stupid White Men*, ReganBooks, New York, 2004 paperback edition, p. 94–97.

Description of the Davison Hotline services: *Free to Be*, Davison, Michigan, March 22, 1977, p. 1.

Hamper on *Flint Voice* as "hippie relic": Ben Hamper, *Rivethead: Tales From the Assembly Line*, Warner Books Inc., New York, 1986, p. 83.

Hamper on *Flint Voice* benefit concerts: Ben Hamper, *Rivethead: Tales From the Assembly Line*, Warner Books Inc., New York, 1986, p. 84.

Hamper on Moore taking chances on people: Shawn Windsor, "Prelude to the Academy Awards: The many roles of Michael Moore," *Detroit Free Press*, February 28, 2004, Saturday 0 Edition, http://www.freep.com/entertainment/movies/moore28_2004022 8.htm.

Description of Moore as cocky: Ben Hamper, *Rivethead: Tales From the Assembly Line*, Warner Books Inc., New York, 1986, p. 85.

Moore attempting to convince Hamper to write: Ben Hamper, *Rivethead: Tales From the Assembly Line*, Warner Books Inc., New York, 1986, p. 86.

Hamper on Bruce Springsteen as the common man: Ben Hamper, *Rivethead: Tales From the Assembly Line*, Warner Books Inc., New York, 1986, p. 196.

Kathleen Glynn on dreams: Larissa MacFarquhar, "The Populist," *The New Yorker*, February 16, 2004, Vol. 80, No. 1, p. 133.

Chapter Three
Are You Going to San Francisco?
Michael Moore at *Mother Jones*

Opening quote regarding U-Haul: Michael Moore, *Roger & Me*, 1989.

Moore's goodbye editorial: Michael Moore, "Goodbye, Friends," *Michigan Voice*, Burton, Michigan, April 1986, p. 59.

Hamper's reaction, "Flint for Frisco?...": Ben Hamper, *Rivethead: Tales From the Assembly Line*, Warner Books Inc., New York, 1986, p. 200.

Introduction of Moore as editor: Adam Hochschild, "Passing the Torch," *Mother Jones*, San Francisco, June 1986, Vol. xi, No. iv, p. 6.

Mother Jones the woman as the mother of the downtrodden: Elliot J. Gorn, "Mother Jones: The Woman," *Mother Jones*, San Francisco, May/June 2001, Vol. 26, No. 3, p. 58. http://www.motherjones.com/news/special_reports/2001/05/mot herjones_gorn.html.

Welcoming Moore to *Mother Jones*: Adam Hochschild, "Passing the Torch," *Mother Jones*, San Francisco, June 1986, Vol. xi, No. iv, p. 6.

Mother Jones' "crass commercialism": Bruce Iwamoto, "Back Talk,"

Mother Jones, San Francisco, July/August 1986, Vol. xi, No. v, p. 4.

Hochschild vs. Moore, rich vs. poor: Alexander Cockburn, "Beat the Devil," *The Nation*, New York, September 13, 1986, Vol. 243, No. 7, p.198.

Don Hazen on Richard Schauffler's dismissal: Alex S. Jones, "Radical Magazine Removes Editor, Setting Off a Widening Political Debate," *New York Times*, New York, Late City Final Edition, September 27, 1986, Section 1, p. 7.

Anonymous source on the Sandinistas article conflict: Emily Schultz, telephone interview, June 24, 2005.

Hochschild letter to *The Nation*: Adam Hochschild, "Letters: Politics?" *The Nation*, New York, October 4, 1986, Vol. 243, No. 10, p. 298.

Hazen, Kollebaum et al., letter to *The Nation*: "Letters: What Politics?" The Nation, New York, October 4, 1986, Vol. 243, No. 10, p. 298.

Moore on Berman's article as Reagan treatise: Alexander Cockburn, "Beat the Devil," *The Nation*, New York, September 13, 1986, Vol. 243, No. 7, p. 198.

Hochschild on Berman and Cockburn feud: Adam Hochschild, "Letters: Politics?" *The Nation*, New York, October 4, 1986, Vol. 243, No. 10, p. 298.

Hochschild on the Sandinistas article: *ibid*.

Hochschild on revolutionary movements: *ibid*.

Hochschild on critical perspectives: *ibid*.

Hochschild on not talking to Cockburn: *ibid*.

Hazen and Kollenbaum letter on Moore's lack of success: *ibid*.

Hazen and Kollenbaum letter on Moore's fall from grace: *ibid*.

Hazen and Kollenbaum letter on Moore's obscuring of his problems: *ibid*.

Hazen and Kollenbaum letter on Moore's problems on the job: *ibid*.

Moore's $2 million suit against *Mother Jones*, and Moore on the magazine damaging itself: Alex S. Jones, "Radical Magazine Removes Editor, Setting Off a Widening Political Debate," *New York Times*, New York, Late City Final Edition, September 27, 1986, Section 1, p. 7.

Anonymous source on Moore's treatment of junior and senior staff:

Emily Schultz, telephone interview, June 24, 2005.

Anonymous source on Moore's tendency to mock: *ibid.*

Anonymous source on the portrayal of the struggle between Moore and Hochschild: *ibid.*

Anonymous source on Moore's later projects: *ibid.*

Anonymous source on the difference in Moore and Hochschild viewpoints of the dismissal conversation: *ibid.*

Cockburn's rebuttal of the Hochschild and Hazen letters, including Schauffler "smears" and definitions of "feud" and "political": Alexander Cockburn, "Cockburn Replies," and "Letters: Politics?" *The Nation*, New York, October 4, 1986, Vol. 243, No. 10, p. 298 and pp. 323–324.

Butler on Moore's tactless attack: *ibid.*

Cockburn's rebuttal of the Hochschild and Hazen letters, regarding the Kennedy story: Alexander Cockburn, "Cockburn Replies," and "Letters: Politics?" *The Nation*, New York, October 4, 1986, Vol. 243, No. 10, p. 298 and pp. 323–324.

Anonymous source on press conference and settlement: Emily Schultz, telephone interview, June 24, 2005.

Mother Jones' junior staff letter: Peggy Lauer, Roberta Williams et al., "Letters: More on Moore," *The Nation*, New York, October 11, 1986, Vol. 243, No. 11, p. 330.

Berman on Moore as "doing Reagan's work": Adam Hochschild, "A Family Fight Hits the Headlines," *Mother Jones*, San Francisco, December 1986, Vol. xi, No. ix, p. 6. Originally appeared in Berman's column in the *Village Voice*.

Hamper's opinion on Moore's firing: Ben Hamper, *Rivethead: Tales From the Assembly Line*, Warner Books Inc., New York, 1986, p. 220.

Anonymous source on Hamper's writing: Emily Schultz, telephone interview, June 24, 2005.

Michael sees discount movies and thanks *Mother Jones* for firing him: Ruthe Stein, "Fighting with Films," *San Francisco Chronicle*, San Francisco, Sunday, June 20, 2004, p. 24. http://sfgate.com/cgibin/article.cgi?file=/chronicle/archive/2004/06/20/PKGJC766UO1.DTL.

Radosh on having had enough of Moore: Daniel Radosh, "Moore Is Less," *Salon*, San Francisco, June 6, 1997, http://www.salon.com/june97/media/media970606.html.

Radosh on Moore's humor: *ibid*.

Radosh on hastening Moore's death: *ibid*.

David Talbot's biography: Warren St. John, "The Salon Makeover," *Wired*, Vol. vii, No. i, January 1999, http://www.wired.com/wired/archive/7.01/talbot.html?pg=1&topic=&topic_set=.

Moore's response to Talbot, including Talbot's resignation from *Mother Jones*: "Moore Fires Back at Salon," *Salon*, San Francisco, July 3, 1997, http://archive.salon.com/july97/moore970703.html.

Moore's response to Radosh, regarding the charmed life: *ibid*.

Moore's response to Radosh, regarding moving into the neighborhood: *ibid*.

Radosh reply to Moore's letter regarding Brooklyn childhood: "Daniel Radosh Responds," *Salon*, San Francisco, July 3, 1997, http://archive.salon.com/july97/moore970703.html.

Talbot reply to Moore's letter regarding corporate malice: "David Talbot Responds," *Salon*, San Francisco, July 3, 1997, http://archive.salon.com/july97/moore970703.html.

Talbot reply to Moore's letter regarding Moore's job hectoring plutocrats: *ibid*.

Talbot reply to Moore's letter regarding Moore's dismissal from *Mother Jones*: *ibid*.

Chapter Four
Out Like Flint
The Bunny Lady, Roger, and Me

Ryan Eashoo on watching *Roger & Me* in Flint: Emily Schultz, telephone interview with Ryan Eashoo, Davison, Michigan, January 20, 2005.

Eashoo on growing up middle class and Flint layoffs: *ibid*.

Moore on *Blood in the Face* and nerve: Michael Moore, commentary, *Roger & Me*, 2003, DVD.

Moore to Alan Poe, Christian Identity minister: Kevin Rafferty, Anne Bohlen, and James Ridgeway, *Blood in the Face*, 1991.

Moore on seeing movies: D.D. Guttenplan, "Suddenly He's In, Unlike

Flint; Michael Moore's Film About Laid-Off Michigan Auto Workers Is Being Promoted, He Notes Ironically, As the Season's 'Feel-Good Hit,'" *Newsday*, New York, December 17, 1989, p. 12.

Moore on hearing about GM plant closures: Michael Moore, commentary, *Roger & Me*, 2003, DVD.

James Musselman on credit in *Roger & Me*: Doron P. Levin, "Maker of Documentary That Attacks G.M. Alienates His Allies," *New York Times*, New York, January 19, 1990, p. C12.

Nader donating office space and seed money: D.D. Guttenplan, "Suddenly He's In, Unlike Flint; Michael Moore's Film About Laid-Off Michigan Auto Workers Is Being Promoted, He Notes Ironically, As the Season's 'Feel-Good Hit,'" *Newsday*, New York, December 17, 1989, p. 12.

Pauline Kael on the offensiveness of *Roger & Me*: Pauline Kael, *Movie Love: Complete Reviews 1988–1991*, New York, Plume, 1991, pp. 242–245.

Moore on San Francisco coffee waitress: Spencer Rumsey, "The New York Newsday Interview With Michael Moore," *Newsday*, New York, January 25, 1990, p. 65.

Moore on riding around in a van with Roger Smith: D.D. Guttenplan, "Suddenly He's In, Unlike Flint; Michael Moore's Film About Laid-Off Michigan Auto Workers is Being Promoted, He Notes Ironically, As the Season's 'Feel-Good Hit,'" *Newsday*, New York, December 17, 1989, p. 12.

Moore on Charlie Chaplin and humor: *ibid*.

Moore on screenings of *Roger & Me* at Telluride: Geoff Hanson, "Michael Moore Returns to Telluride," Telluride Film Festival, September 1992, http://www.michaelmoore.com/dogeatdogfilms/films/telluride.html.

Moore on generosity of sound lab Du Art: Michael Moore, commentary, *Roger & Me*, 2003, DVD.

Moore on getting to Telluride: Geoff Hanson, "Michael Moore Returns to Telluride," Telluride Film Festival, September 1992, http://www.michaelmoore.com/dogeatdogfilms/films/telluride.html.

Moore on people laughing during the titles: *ibid*.

Moore on not going home for eleven months: *ibid*.

Moore on riding in a limo: D.D. Guttenplan, "Suddenly He's In, Unlike Flint; Michael Moore's Film About Laid-Off Michigan Auto Workers Is Being Promoted, He Notes Ironically, As the Season's 'Feel-Good Hit,'" *Newsday*, New York, December 17, 1989, p. 12.

Moore on the facts in *Roger & Me*: Spencer Rumsey, "The New York Newsday Interview With Michael Moore," *Newsday*, New York, January 25, 1990, p. 65.

Pauline Kael on Moore's broad questions: Pauline Kael, *Movie Love: Complete Reviews 1988–1991*, New York, Plume, 1991, pp. 242–245

Pauline Kael on not believing Moore: *ibid.*

Moore on Kael having to travel to New York to see his movie: Michael Moore, "Pauline Kael, the Truth, and Nothing But... Brought to You by AOL Time Warner," January 12, 2000, http://www.michaelmoore.com/words/message/index.php?messageDate=2000-01-12.

Ebert on the "success ethic": Roger Ebert, "Attacks on 'Roger & Me' completely miss point of film," *Chicago Sun Times*, February 11, 1990, http://rogerebert.suntimes.com/apps/pbcs.dll/article?AID=/19900211/COMMENTARY/22010306/1023.

Ebert on Moore thumbing his nose at GM: *ibid.*

Ebert on the poetry and humor *Roger & Me* supplied: *ibid.*

Ed Lachman on documentaries and chronology: *ibid.*

Karen Thorson on critics: *ibid.*

Richard Bernstein on *Roger & Me* as a David and Goliath story: "'Roger & Me': Documentary? Satire? Or Both?" *New York Times*, New York, February 1, 1990, p. C20.

Bernstein on the rules of a documentary: *ibid.*

Bernstein on the title of *Roger & Me*: *ibid.*

Vacant homes in Flint: Francis X. Donnelly and Dale G. Young, "GM's desertion decimates Flint: Closed plants, anemic tax base strip city services," *Detroit News*, Detroit, July 23, 2002, Autos Insider, http://www.detnews.com/2002/autosinsider/0207/29/a01-544821.htm.

Amount of judgment awarded to Stecco: Genesee County Circuit Court, Michigan, Online Court Records, Case No. 90-005047-NZ,

http://www.co.genesee.mi.us/circuitcourt/New%20web%20site/
home.htm#.

Flint cut backs: *ibid.*

Moore on number of votes held by head of GM: Michael Moore, "A
Final Election Day Letter," November 7, 2000,
http://www.michaelmoore.com/words/message/index.php?mess
ageDate=2000-11-07.

Eashoo in believing in Moore: Emily Schultz, telephone interview
with Ryan Eashoo, Davison, Michigan, January 20, 2005.

Eashoo on Moore taking a stab at Flint: *ibid.*

Chapter Five
So Long AutoWorld, Hello *TV Nation*

John Derevlany on *TV Nation*'s first season: Emily Schultz, E-mail
interview with John Derevlany, February 10, 2005.

Amount lost to corporate crime: Michael Moore and Kathleen
Glynn, *Adventures in a TV Nation: The Stories Behind America's
Most Outrageous TV Show*, HarperPerennial, New York, 1998, p. 47.

Derevlany on the formation of the Crackers mascot: Emily Schultz,
E-mail interview with John Derevlany, February 10, 2005.

Derevlany on the lack of visual impact of corporate crime stories: *ibid.*

Widgery and Associates polls: Michael Moore and Kathleen Glynn,
*Adventures in a TV Nation: The Stories Behind America's Most
Outrageous TV Show*, HarperPerennial, New York, 1998, p. 205
and p. 207.

Moore on breaking the rules of TV: Karen Duffy, "The Moore, the
merrier — director Michael Moore," *Interview*, New York,
September 1994, Vol. 24, No. 9, pp. 70–72.

Moore on answering the same questions: Michael Moore, "Roger
and I, Off to Hollywood and Home to Flint," *New York Times*,
New York, July 15, 1990, p. H11.

Moore on different questions: *ibid.*

Moore on shopping in Flint: "Talk of the Town — Success," *The New
Yorker*, October 12, 1992, Vol. 68, No. 34, pp. 44–46.

Moore on instant granting: Ron Sheldon, "Exclusive Interview with

Michael Moore of TV Nation," *People's Weekly World*, New York, September 23, 1995, http://www.pww.org/archives95/ 95-09-23-3.html.

Moore on the status of black filmmakers in Hollywood: *ibid.*

Moore on bombing in Iraq starting while he was at Sundance: *ibid.*

Moore on approaching John Sayles to present a political stance: *ibid.*

Moore on having his work cut out for him: *ibid.*

Moore on types of wars and the lessons of Vietnam: *ibid.*

Moore on liberal television and liberals in general: Michael Moore and Kathleen Glynn, *Adventures in a TV Nation: The Stories Behind America's Most Outrageous TV Show*, HarperPerennial, New York, 1998, p. 4.

Moore on employing Ben Hamper: Karen Duffy, "The Moore, the merrier — director Michael Moore," *Interview*, New York, September 1994, Vol. 24, No. 9, pp. 70–72.

Derevlany on the comedy/politics divide of *TV Nation*: Emily Schultz, E-mail interview with John Derevlany, February 10, 2005.

Derevlany on his Comedy Central experience: *ibid.*

Moore on the importance of casting a script: Justin Smallbridge, "Canada and Me: Michael Moore switches his sights from Flint, Michigan to a fictional feature poking fun at Canadian anxiety about big brother USA" *The Globe and Mail*, December 31, 1993, p. AL1.

Walter Gasparovic on Canadian Bacon production and humor on the set: Emily Schultz, E-mail interview with Walter Gasparovic, March 8, 2005.

Moore on nonfiction versus fiction, television versus film: David Sterritt, "One Filmmaker's Answer to Apathy," *Christian Science Monitor*, Boston, October 2, 1995, Vol. 87, No. 215, p. 13.

Moore and Glynn on behaving without heed of working in television again: Michael Moore and Kathleen Glynn, *Adventures in a TV Nation: The Stories Behind America's Most Outrageous TV Show*, HarperPerennial, New York, 1998, p. 12.

Moore and Glynn on not lying to the viewer: *ibid.*

Derevlany on Moore's advice against career angling: Emily Schultz, E-mail interview with John Derevlany, February 10, 2005.

Derevlany on pitching ideas to *TV Nation*: *ibid.*

Derevlany on going to New York: *ibid.*

Derevlany on assigning segments: *ibid.*

Derevlany on scripts, improvisation, and directing: *ibid.*

Derevlany on replacing the original Crackers actor: *ibid.*

Derevlany on the Crackers costume: *ibid.*

Derevlany on "suit performers": *ibid.*

Derevlany on suit solutions: *ibid.*

Derevlany on driving the Crackers mobile: *ibid.*

Derevlany on long hours: *ibid.*

Derevlany on the baseball stadium appearance: *ibid.*

Derevlany on punk and playing rough: *ibid.*

Derevlany on physically fighting with the management of striking
    Detroit newspapers: *ibid.*

Derevlany on his injuries: *ibid.*

Moore on the difficulty of the show: David Hirning, "Michael
    Moore," *Washington Free Press*, Seattle, September/October 1996,
    Issue No. 23, http://www.washingtonfreepress.org/23/Q&A.html.

Derevlany on dubbing lines in post-production: Emily Schultz,
    E-mail interview with John Derevlany, February 10, 2005.

Moore and Glynn on government regulations pertaining to water:
    Michael Moore and Kathleen Glynn, *Adventures in a TV Nation:
    The Stories Behind America's Most Outrageous TV Show*,
    HarperPerennial, New York, 1998, p. 25.

Moore and Glynn on the "Lie of the Week" segment: *ibid*, p. 9.

Moore lured away from NBC: Chip Rowe, "A Funny, Subversive '60
    Minutes,'" *American Journalism Review*, Maryland, July/August
    1995, http://www.ajr.org/Article.asp?id=2125.

Moore on the Fox network strictness: David Hirning, "Michael
    Moore," *Washington Free Press*, Seattle, Washington,
    September/October 1996, Issue No. 23,
    http://www.washingtonfreepress.org/23/Q&A.html.

Marvin Kitman on *TV Nation*'s censored abortion segment:
    Marvin Kitman, "'TV Nation' Facing Fox Fire: Will the network
    executives get Michael Moore's humor?", *Newsday*, New York,
    July 20, 1995, p. B69.

Lynn Elber on Secret Service reviewing *TV Nation*: Lynn Elber,
    "Secret Service Seeks Review of Abortion Foe's Unaired TV

Interview," Associated Press, Pasadena, California, January 16, 1995.

Secret Service Harnischfeger on context: *ibid.*

Roy McMillan on hypothetical and leading questions: *ibid.*

Kevin Mattson on cynicism in *Canadian Bacon*: Kevin Mattson, "The Perils of Michael Moore Political Criticism in an Age of Entertainment," *Dissent Magazine*, New York, Spring 2003, Vol. 50, No. 2, http://www.dissentmagazine.org/menutest/articles/sp03/mattson.htm.

Mattson on "hipness unto death": *ibid.*

Tom Shales on Moore's lack of noble calling: Tom Shales, "TV Preview — 'Nation' With Malice Toward All," *Washington Post*, Washington, D.C., July 19, 1994, p. B1.

James Ledbetter on Moore's lack of evolution: Chip Rowe, "A Funny, Subversive '60 Minutes,'" *American Journalism Review*, Maryland, July/August 1995, http://www.ajr.org/Article.asp?id=2125.

Mattson on making political criticism entertaining: Kevin Mattson, "The Perils of Michael Moore Political Criticism in an Age of Entertainment," *Dissent Magazine*, New York, Spring 2003, Vol. 50, No. 2, http://www.dissentmagazine.org/menutest/articles/sp03/mattson.htm.

Moore on the pessimism in *Canadian Bacon*: Ron Sheldon, "Exclusive Interview with Michael Moore of TV Nation," *People's Weekly World*, New York, September 23, 1995, http://www.pww.org/archives95/95-09-23-3.html

Gasparovic on working with John Candy: Emily Schultz, E-mail interview with Walter Gasparovic, March 8, 2005.

Moore on studio bosses exploiting as much John Candy material as possible: David Sterritt, "One Filmmaker's Answer to Apathy," *Christian Science Monitor*, Boston, October 2, 1995, Vol. 87, No. 215, p. 13.

Gasparovic on differences between Moore and the studio: Emily Schultz, E-mail interview with Walter Gasparovic, March 8, 2005.

Derevlany on Moore as brilliant and inspiring: Emily Schultz, E-mail interview with John Derevlany, February 10, 2005.

Derevlany on prank shows: *ibid.*

Chapter Six
Biggie Up the Downsize
Book Signings, Road Food, and Nike

Moore on being out of work and writing a book: Michael Moore, *The Big One*, 1997.

Moore on writing and the cancellation of *TV Nation*: David Hirning, "Michael Moore," *Washington Free Press*, Seattle, September/ October 1996, Issue No. 23, http://www.washingtonfreepress.org/23/Q&A.html.

Moore on seeing something different in America's cities: Michael Fleming, "Dish — Disney Bug-eyed; Big bows; Selleck choosy," *Variety*, Los Angeles, June 17, 1997, p. 39.

Moore as the put-on Everyman: Anita Gates, "Book Review Desk: How the Other Half Lives," *New York Times*, December 29, 1996, Late Edition, Final, Section 7, p. 11.

Moore on making the *New York Times* bestseller list: Michael Moore, *The Big One*, 1997.

Moore on Ani DiFranco and the shaven armpit: Ian Hodder, "Michael Moore's Ongoing Crusade Against Corporate Greed Won him an Audience with Big, Bad Nike," *Industry Central: The Motion Picture and Television Industry's First Stop!*, California, http://industrycentral.net/director_interviews/MM02.HTM.

Moore on talking to P.R. people: *ibid.*

Moore on defending layoffs during record profits: *ibid.*

Moore on "What Is Terrorism?": Michael Moore, *The Big One*, 1997.

Moore on the company as a murderer: Michael Moore, *The Big One*, 1997.

Mary Gielow on Moore's book tour: Michael Moore, *The Big One*, 1997.

Moore on keeping the camera running: Michael Moore, *The Big One*, 1997.

Moore on not crossing the picket line: photo caption, *Philadelphia Inquirer*, September 12, 1996, p. B1.

Jody Kohn on Moore's encouragement of shopping elsewhere: Michael Wines, "An Odd Rift Develops Between an Author and Borders, a Chain Promoting His Book," *New York Times*, New York, November 18, 1996, Late Edition, Final, Section D, p. 10.

Moore on his Borders Books World Trade Center stop: *ibid.*

Moore on directives from Borders corporate headquarters: *ibid.*

Moore on not going out on a "union organizing tour": *ibid.*

Moore on "Moore Is Less": "Moore fires back at Salon," *Salon*, San
     Francisco, July 3, 1997,
     http://archive.salon.com/july97/moore970703.html.

Moore on *Salon*'s affiliation with Borders: *ibid.*

Radosh on "Five Reasons the Left Can Do without Michael Moore":
     Daniel Radosh, "Moore is Less," *Salon*, San Francisco, June 6,
     1997, http://www.salon.com/june97/media/media970606.html.

Talbot on connection between *Salon* and Borders: "David Talbot
     responds," *Salon*, San Francisco, July 3, 1997,
     http://archive.salon.com/july97/moore970703.html.

Talbot on Moore swinging wildly: *ibid.*

Review of *The Big One*: Janet Maslin, "A Sly Lens on Corporate
     America," *New York Times*, New York, April 10, 1998, Late
     Edition, Final, Section E, p. 1.

Moore on Phil Knight rarely giving interviews: Monica Roman,
     "Independent's Day: IFP skeds 400 pix for eclectic fest," *Variety*,
     Los Angeles, July 16, 1997, p. 10.

Knight on the shoe factory in the sky: Michael Moore, *The Big One*, 1997.

Review calling *The Big One* "a lively sparring match": Janet Maslin,
     "A Sly Lens on Corporate America," *New York Times*, New York,
     April 10, 1998, Late Edition, Final, Section E, p. 1.

Moore on Nike seeing a bootleg of *The Big One*: Ian Hodder,
     "Michael Moore's Ongoing Crusade Against Corporate Greed
     Won him an Audience with Big, Bad Nike," *Industry Central: The
     Motion Picture and Television Industry's First Stop!*, California,
     http://industrycentral.net/director_interviews/MM02.HTM.

Moore on going out to breakfast with Nike director of public rela-
     tions: *ibid.*

Moore on adding a scene to the movie: *ibid.*

Moore on Knight and subtle racism: *ibid.*

Mattson on "Moore's next bit of entertainment": Kevin Mattson,
     "The Perils of Michael Moore Political Criticism in an Age of
     Entertainment," *Dissent Magazine*, New York, Spring 2003, Vol.
     50, No. 2, http://www.dissentmagazine.org/menutest/articles/

sp03/mattson.htm.

Moore speech at the Bagdad Theater in Portland, Oregon: Josh Feit, "Michael & Me: The Director of The Big One Brings his Entertaining Attack on 'Economic Terrorism' to Phil Knight's Backyard," *Willamette Week*, Portland, Oregon, April 1, 1998, http://www.wweek.com/html/moore040198.html.

Portland audience's questions: *ibid.*

Nike on falling stock prices: John H. Cushman Jr., "Nike Pledges to End Child Labor and Apply U.S. Rules Abroad," *New York Times*, New York, May 13, 1998, Late Edition, Final, Section D, p. 1.

Knight on material impact on Nike sales: *ibid.*

Germany's love of Moore: Steven Zeitchik, "Michael Moore: The New JFK?" *Publishers Weekly*, October 27, 2003, p. 15. http://www.publishersweekly.com/article/CA330965.html?text=Downsize+This.

German foreword for *Downsize This!*: *ibid.*

Chapter Seven
The Awful Truth of Working in Television

Moore on the original *Awful Truth* movie poster: Michael Moore, commentary, *The Awful Truth*, 2003, DVD.

Ed Carroll on Moore: Richard Katz, "Bravo Claims Moore Series," *Variety*, Los Angeles, November 11, 1998, p. 8.

Edelstein on the Academy Award nomination and hiring at *The Awful Truth*: Emily Schultz, telephone interview with Alan Edelstein, New York, March 7, 2005.

Edelstein on not being anti-Michael Moore: *ibid.*

Edelstein on the pace of television work: *ibid.*

Edelstein on Moore's reputation: *ibid.*

Edelstein on his assigned segments: *ibid.*

Edelstein on placing the Taliban segment: *ibid.*

Edelstein on his dismissal from *The Awful Truth*: *ibid.*

Lucianne Goldberg "LucyCam" Web site text: "Arts and Entertainment: Michael Moore," Playboy Enterprises, Chicago, 1999, http://www.playboyenterprises.com/home/content.cfm?content=t_title_as_division&ArtTypeID=0008B752-BBD0-1C76-8FEA8304E50A010D&packet=000B8140-7874-1C7A-9

B578304E50A011A&MmenuFlag=foundation&viewMe=4.

Edelstein's visits to Moore: John Tierney, "The Big City: When Tables Turn, Knives Come Out," *New York Times*, New York, June 17, 2000, p. B1.

Edelstein on his competence: Emily Schultz, telephone interview with Alan Edelstein, New York, March 7, 2005.

Edelstein on engaging in satirical activity: *ibid*.

Edelstein on banter with Moore and acting out of character: *ibid*.

Edelstein on his nonbeliever's journey: *ibid*.

Edelstein on Moore as a prop: *ibid*.

Moore on Edelstein as a disgruntled employee: John Tierney, "The Big City: When Tables Turn, Knives Come Out," *New York Times*, New York, June 17, 2000, p. B1.

Kyra Vogt from Moore's office on Edelstein: *ibid*.

Edelstein on the plea bargain: Emily Schultz, telephone interview with Alan Edelstein, New York, March 7, 2005.

Edelstein on truth, falsehood, and a game of chicken: *ibid*.

Glynn on the comedy ghetto: Larissa MacFarquhar, "The Populist," *The New Yorker*, New York, February 16, 2004, Vol. 80, No. 1, p. 133.

Derevlany on Glynn's role as producer of *TV Nation*: Emily Schultz, E-mail interview with John Derevlany, February 10, 2005.

Eric Zicklin on Moore giving people chances: Larissa MacFarquhar, "The Populist," *The New Yorker*, New York, February 16, 2004, Vol. 80, No. 1, p. 133.

Zicklin on Moore as a media product: *ibid*.

Chris Kelly on having his heart broken by Moore: *ibid*.

Moore on apologizing: *ibid*.

Karen Duffy on the left cannibalizing itself: *ibid*.

Caryn James on willfully rude entertainment: Caryn James, "TV Weekend; Cutups on Cable: Odd Ones In," *New York Times*, New York, April 30, 1999, p. E1.

James on the lunacy of living in a corporate culture: *ibid*.

The Playboy Foundation on the humor and satire of *The Awful Truth*: "Arts and Entertainment: Michael Moore," Playboy Enterprises, Chicago, 1999, http://www.playboyenterprises.com/home/content.cfm?content=t_title_as_division&ArtTypeID=0008B752-BBD0-1C76-8FEA

8304E50A010D&packet=000B8140-7874-1C7A-
9B578304E50A011A&MmenuFlag=foundation&viewMe=4.

Moore on ideas from the bottom up: Michael Moore, commentary,
The Awful Truth, 2003, DVD.

Moore on disbelief of Chris Jones in the mosh pit: Michael Moore,
commentary, *The Awful Truth*, 2003, DVD.

Moore on Alan Keyes in the mosh pit: *ibid.*

Moore on the media attention brought on by the mosh pit incident:
ibid.

Alan Keyes on the mosh pit as an emblem of democracy: Gail
Collins, "Public Interests: Dignity, Always Dignity," *New York
Times*, New York, January 28, 2000, p. A23.

Moore on the debating of the mosh pit: Michael Moore, commentary, *The Awful Truth*, 2003, DVD.

Collins on Presidential decorum: Gail Collins, "Public Interests;
Dignity, Always Dignity," *New York Times*, New York, January 28,
2000, p. A23.

Collins on Presidential underwear preferences: *ibid.*

Moore on being restrained by police during Rage Against the
Machine video shoot: Michael Moore, "The Machine Raged On
Me," December 12, 2000, http://www.michaelmoore.com/words/
message/index.php?messageDate=2000-12-12.

The Awful Truth on voting for Alan Keyes: Michael Moore, *The
Awful Truth*, 2000.

Moore on positive response from Harlem: Michael Moore, commentary, *The Awful Truth*, 2003, DVD.

Moore about being right and forging on: Andrew Collins, "Michael
Moore: U.S. Comedian and Documentary-maker Michael
Moore Explains his Thinking on Gun Control, American
Foreign Policy, and Making Movies to Eat Popcorn To,"
Guardian, London, November 11, 2002,
http://film.guardian.co.uk/interview/interview-
pages/0,6737,841083,00.html.

Moore on Catholic upbringing and bailing with a Dixie cup: *ibid.*

Moore on lack of hope for the United States: *ibid.*

Edelstein on Moore as a character: Emily Schultz, telephone
interview with Alan Edelstein, New York, March 7, 2005.

Chapter Eight
Gun Crazy
Bowling for Success

Moore on the image from the Columbine tragedy that affected him most: Michael Moore, "Return to Denver/Littleton" featurette, *Bowling for Columbine*, 2003, DVD.

Moore on what a violent country the United States is: *ibid.*

The why behind the Columbine tragedy: Dave Cullen, "Inside the Columbine High Investigation: Everything You Know About the Littleton Killings Is Wrong," *Salon*, San Francisco, September 23, 1999, http://www.salon.com/news/feature/1999/09/23/columbine/index.html.

Moore on the Buell area as "Flint's dump": Michael Moore, "About Flint," March 1, 2000, http://www.michaelmoore.com/words/message/index.php?messageDate=2000-03-01.

Moore on Buell being close to where Glynn grew up: *ibid.*

Arthur Busch on Buell poverty: Dee-Ann Durban, Associated Press, "Michigan Community Still Not Over Shooting," Mount Morris Township, Michigan, March 31, 2005. See also: http://www.wtopnews.com/index.php?nid=316&sid=432318.

Moore on claiming the NRA presidency: Andrew Collins, "Michael Moore: U.S. Comedian and Documentary-maker Michael Moore Explains his Thinking on Gun Control, American Foreign Policy, and Making Movies to Eat Popcorn To," *Guardian*, London, November 11, 2002, http://film.guardian.co.uk/interview/interviewpages/0,6737,841083,00.html.

Moore on continuing to be an NRA member: *ibid.*

Moore on ringing Charlton Heston's buzzer: Andrew Collins, "Michael Moore : U.S. Comedian and Documentary-maker Michael Moore Explains his Thinking on Gun Control, American Foreign Policy, and Making Movies to Eat Popcorn To," *Guardian*, London, November 11, 2002, Part Two, http://film.guardian. co.u/interview/interviewpages/0,6737,841083,00.html.

Moore on being locked in Heston's garden: Michael Moore, "Film Festival Scrapbook," Cannes, *Bowling for Columbine*, 2003, DVD.

Moore on taking his "licks": *ibid.*

Moore on not feeling sorry for Heston: Andrew Collins, "Michael Moore: U.S. Comedian and Documentary-maker Michael Moore Explains his Thinking on Gun Control, American Foreign Policy, and Making Movies to Eat Popcorn To," *Guardian*, London, November 11, 2002, http://film.guardian.co.uk/interview/interviewpages/0,6737,841083,00.html.

Edelstein on Moore as a failed priest: Emily Schultz, telephone interview with Alan Edelstein, New York, March 7, 2005.

Collins on authorship in Moore's films: Andrew Collins, "Michael Moore: U.S. Comedian and Documentary-maker Michael Moore Explains his Thinking on Gun Control, American Foreign Policy, and Making Movies to Eat Popcorn To," *Guardian*, London, November 11, 2002, http://film.guardian.co.uk/interview/interviewpages/0,6737,841083,00.html.

Gus Van Sant on being a fan of *Bowling for Columbine*: Nev Pierce, "Gus Van Sant: Elephant," *BBC Film*, 2004, http://www.bbc.co.uk/films/2004/01/28/gus_van_sant_elephant_interview.shtml.

Gus Van Sant on the differences between his film *Elephant* and *Bowling for Columbine*: *ibid.*

Moore on interviewing James Nichols: Andrew Collins, "Michael Moore: US comedian and documentary-maker Michael Moore explains his thinking on gun control, American foreign policy, and making movies to eat popcorn to," *Guardian*, London, November 11, 2002, http://film.guardian.co.uk/interview/interviewpages/0,6737,841083,00.html.

Lisa Herling of HarperCollins on political books: Eric Demby, "Angry White Men: Michael Moore, Noam Chomsky, and Greg Palast Hit Bestseller List With Incendiary Books," *Village Voice*, New York, August 21–27, 2002, Vol. 47, No. 34, p. 57. http://www.villagevoice.com/news/0234,demby,37600,1.html.

Moore on Mr. and Mrs. America: *ibid.*

Moore on his mother: Michael Moore, "With my mom at the Hudson River, Thanksgiving 2001," August 5, 2002, http://www.michaelmoore.com/special/mom.php.

Moore on panic of winning Academy Award: Michael Moore, "Exclusive Michael Moore Interview on his Oscar Win and Acceptance Speech," *Bowling for Columbine*, 2003, DVD.

Moore Academy Award speech: Michael Moore, *BBC News*, March 24, 2003, http://news.bbc.co.uk/1/hi/entertainment/film/2879857.stm.

Moore on having a great Oscar moment: Michael Moore, "Exclusive Michael Moore Interview on his Oscar Win and Acceptance Speech," *Bowling for Columbine*, 2003, DVD.

Moore to media about telling the truth: Caroline Overington, "I'd like to thank George for making me angry," *Sydney Morning Herald*, Sydney, March 25, 2003, http://www.smh.com.au/articles/2003/03/24/1048354548057.html.

Moore on appropriateness of his speech: Michael Moore, "Exclusive Michael Moore Interview on his Oscar Win and Acceptance Speech," *Bowling for Columbine*, 2003, DVD.

Chapter Nine
Moore Smokes 'Em Out
Fahrenheit 9/11

Moore on being dropped by Walt Disney Company: Michael Moore, "When You Wish Upon A Star..." May 7, 2004, http://www.michaelmoore.com/words/message/index.php?messageDate=2004-05-07.

Moore on leaving himself out of *Fahrenheit 9/11*: Gary Strauss, "The Truth about Michael Moore," *USA Today*, New York, June 21, 2004, p.1D. http://www.usatoday.com/life/movies/news/2004-06-20-moore_x.htm.

Moore on body image and appearing blown-up on a movie screen: Anthony Ha, "Michael Moore: Kiss kiss, bang bang," *The Stanford Daily*, Stanford, California, October 18, 2002, http://daily.stanford.org/tempo?page=content&id=9113&repository=0001_article.

Moore on six million dollars of Disney money: Michael Moore, "When You Wish Upon A Star..." May 7, 2004, http://www.michaelmoore.com/words/message/index.php?mess

ageDate=2004-05-07.

George Gittoes on use of his scenes by Moore: "Fed: Aust Filmmaker Objects to Moore Use of Film Segments," Australian Associated Press, July 27, 2004. See also: http://www.theage.com.au/articles/2004/07/27/ 1090693936198.html?oneclick=true.

George Gittoes on legal agreement with Moore: "Redemption Song," *Filmink*, 2005, http://www.filmink.com.au/disc/ default.asp?subsection=1.

Bush must answer to Lila Lipscomb: A.O. Scott, "Unruly Scorn Leaves Room for Restraint But Not a Lot," *New York Times*, June 23, 2004, p. E1.

Fahrenheit 9/11 and subtlety in American politics: Luis H. Francia, "Michael Moore — On Stage and In Person!" *Village Voice*, New York, September 8–14, 2004, Vol. 49, No. 36, p. C57.

Fahrenheit 9/11 as an indispensable document of its time: A.O. Scott, "Unruly Scorn Leaves Room for Restraint But Not a Lot," *New York Times*, New York, June 23, 2004, p. E1.

Fahrenheit 9/11's persuasion to reexamine assumptions: *ibid.*

Harlan Jacobson on *Fahrenheit 9/11*: Gary Strauss, "The Truth about Michael Moore," *USA Today*, New York, June 21, 2004, p. 1D. http://www.usatoday.com/life/movies/news/2004-06-20-moore_x.htm.

Joyce Wadler on Moore's schlumpy image: Joyce Wadler with Paula Schwartz and Melena Z. Ryzik, "Boldface Names," *New York Times*, New York, June 16, 2004, Late Edition, Final, Section B, p. 2.

Moore on his fact-checking "war room" and attempts to libel him: Philip Sheldon, "Michael Moore Is Ready for His Close-Up," *New York Times*, New York, June 20, 2004, Late Edition, Final, Section 2, p. 1.

Fahrenheit 9/11 opinions from the executive office and first lady: Michael Moore, "The Release of *Fahrenheit 9/11*" featurette, *Fahrenheit 9/11*, 2004, DVD.

David Bossie on *Fahrenheit 9/11*: Hanna Rosin and Mike Allen, "*Fahrenheit 9/11* Is a Red-Hot Ticket," *Washington Post*, Washington, D.C., June 24, 2004, p. A1. http://www.washingtonpost.com/wp-dyn/articles/

A849-2004Jun23.html.

Richard Goldstein on ABC and NBC reaction to *Fahrenheit 9/11*:
Richard Goldstein, "Mauling Michael Moore, The attack on
Fahrenheit 9/11: Fox lays back while ABC and NBC pile on,"
Village Voice, New York, June 23–29, 2004, Vol. 49, No. 25, p. 66.
http://www.villagevoice.com/news/0426,goldstein,54689,6.html.

Goldstein and the power of the media: *ibid*.

Kerry campaign and "Michael Moore baggage": Hanna Rosin and
Mike Allen, "*Fahrenheit 9/11* Is a Red-Hot Ticket," *Washington
Post*, Washington, D.C., June 24, 2004, p. A1.
http://www.washingtonpost.com/wp-dyn/articles/
A849-2004Jun23.html.

Conclusion
Citizen Moore

Moore on John Kerry not being you or me: Michael Moore, "One
Day Left," November 1, 2004,
http://www.michaelmoore.com/words/message/index.php?mess
ageDate=2004-11-01.

Errol Morris on liberal agenda: Nancy Ramsy, "Politically Inclined
Filmmakers Say There Is Life After the Election," *New York
Times*, New York, December 27, 2004, Late Edition, final, Section
E, p. 3. See also:
http://www.errolmorris.com/content/news/nyt_ramsey.html.

Voters under age 30: David C. King, "Youth Came Through With Big
Turnout," *The Boston Globe*, Boston, November 4, 2004, p. A15.
http://www.boston.com/news/globe/editorial_opinion/oped/arti
cles/2004/11/04/youth_came_through_with_big_turnout/.

Moore on House and Senate together: Michael Moore, "In the
Clearing Stands a Boxer ... a Letter from Michael Moore,"
January 7, 2005, http://www.michaelmoore.com/words/
message/index.php?messageDate=2005-01-07.

Representative Maxine Waters on Moore educating young voters:
ibid.